Praise for *The Journey of Janell*

"Mike is one of the most competent and genuine peak performance coaches I know. We have walked through life together for 25 years. This uplifting book is full of amazing wisdom and guidance that will inspire and equip you as you continue to seek your dreams on this grand sacred journey!"

— David L. Cook, PhD, Peak Performance Coach, Author "Seven Days in Utopia" and "greatness," Executive Producer and screenwriter "Seven Days in Utopia"

"Mike Van Hoozer has spent a lifetime helping athletes understand that the most important battles in sports and in life are rarely physical – they are fought in the mind and won in the heart. In The Journey of Janell, Mike does something special. He tells a story that reminds us that true greatness isn't measured by trophies or scorecards, but by the character we build and the lives we lift along the way.

Janell's story is one of grit, grace, faith, and purpose, and Mike guides the reader through her story with the wisdom of a coach who understands that sport is one of life's greatest classrooms.

If you are an athlete, coach, business leader, parent, or anyone striving to live with intention, The Journey of Janell will encourage you to pursue excellence not just in performance, but in the way you live, serve, and lead."

— Spencer Tillman, Super Bowl Champion, Collegiate National Champion, and College Football Analyst, FOX Sports

*"Mike is a trusted friend and mentor who has personally invested in my volleyball program over the last few years. So much of my team's mental game is built upon Mike's Keys to a Championship Mindset. **The Journey of Janell** is an in-depth look at the wisdom he has brought to my team and to so many others...wisdom that not only applies to growing athletes in sports, but to growing leaders in everyday life."*

— Sydney Zimmerman, Head Volleyball Coach, Churchill Fulshear High School

"Once again, Mike Van Hoozer gives us some of the most practical tools for our journey as he honors an incredible athlete, Janell Lysack Joslin. Whatever your game, Mike's ability to distill life-changing principles will elevate your life and leadership. He's a great coach and storyteller, and I know it is one of the great honors of his life to have both coached Janell, and to share her story with the world."

— Roger Patterson, Senior Pastor, CityRise Church, Houston, TX, and Author of *40 Days of Faith*

"I am blessed to call Mike both a brother and a friend. I was also blessed to know Janell through our years of service in the FCA ministry. Her personality and spirit for the Lord and for people were infectious, her competitive spirit was fierce, and her focus was laser like. My hope is that The Journey of Janell, through Mike's pen, not only will help you develop keys to a championship mindset in all areas of life, but I pray also that Janell's life blesses, inspires, and even challenges you to grow and bear much fruit. Thank you, Mike, for your faithfulness and utilizing your leadership and coaching gifts in such a necessary space that many of us often ignore. Finally, thank you for sharing Janell's journey with us. Blessings my brother!"

— Mikado Hinson, Chaplain, Houston, Texans

"Life is full of moments, both good and tough ones. Mike's ability to help others work through the mental side of these times has paid dividends for me and so many of my players. I have seen firsthand the impact his teaching has had on dozens of high school athletes – supplying them with the tools needed to stay in a healthy mental capacity within an environment where stresses pop up constantly. The idea of performance not being tied to their identity is so powerful to these young minds! This book allows us to embrace the process and the moments along the way."

— Shannon Heston, Head Boys' Basketball Coach, Seven Lakes High School

"The Journey of Janell is an inspiring story of a young golfer aiming to reach her peak performance and how Mike Van Hoozer helped her maximize her potential in golf and life. I have worked with Mike personally to improve my own running performance, and his strategies have been very effective for me in my running career as well as my life outside of running. Mike is a joy to work with, and this book shows the special relationships that he builds with his clientele to help them be their best."

— Catherine Kruppa, MS, RD, CSSD, LD, Registered Dietitian. Board Certified, Specialist in Sports Dietetics and Certified Wellness Coach, Advice for Eating - Nutrition and Wellness Consulting

"Mike is a true leader who inspires everyone who comes across his path. I've known him for more than a decade and have witnessed his ability to lead with vision, clarity, and humility. He is kind, thoughtful, and purposeful with a story that will touch your heart and light your soul with passion as you take your own journey to accomplish the will of Almighty God!"

— Keith Garvin, MAA, Emmy & Murrow Award-Winning broadcast journalist

"I have known Mike for more than 35 years as a colleague and trusted source of wisdom and encouragement. I've had the privilege of watching the ideas behind this book develop over time - grounded in the belief that a championship mindset begins with believing transformation is possible. Through a powerful and inspiring story, Mike brings those principles to life in a way that will encourage anyone striving to perform and live with purpose."

— Terrence Gee, Chief Information Officer, Rice University

"I was blessed to work with the Janell who had been through the crucible and come through it as an unstoppable force at Callaway Golf. She proved time after time as we battled through difficult moments that she simply could not be overrun because of the mental and emotional "steel" that Mike had forged in her."

— Brad Barnett, Vice President, Operations, Callaway Golf

"My partnership with Mike was extremely useful! In the life of an NFL kicker, I have had to look deep within myself to find out where I find my acceptance from. In addition to my faith journey, Mike shared the 5 keys to a championship mindset found in this book and helped me organize my thoughts in a deliberate manner to discover that my value was in being a child of God before being an athlete. I was able to swing free with confidence knowing that the battle has already been won. I GET to praise the Lord through my preparation, hard work, and performance on and off the field...by the grace of God."

— Riley Patterson, NFL Kicker

THE Journey OF Janell

A story of
grit and *grace*

MIKE VAN HOOZER

Published in Fulshear, TX by Hoozer House Press.

Paperback ISBN: 979-8-9948673-2-7
Hardcover ISBN: 979-8-9948673-3-4
eBook ISBN: 979-8-9948673-1-0

Printed in the United States of America First Edition: 2026

Library of Congress Cataloging-in-Publication Data

Names: Van Hoozer, Mike, author.
Title: The journey of Janell : a story of grit and grace / Mike Van Hoozer.
Description: First edition. | Fulshear, TX : Hoozer House Press, [2026]
Identifiers: LCCN: 2026908016 | ISBN: 9798994867327 (Paperback) | 9798994867334 (Hardcover) | 9798994867310 (eBook)
Subjects: LCSH: Joslin, Janell Marie Lysack. | Sports--Psychological aspects. | Coaching (Athletics)-- Psychological aspects. | Teenage girls--Conduct of life. | Leadership. | Success--Psychological aspects. | Resilience (Psychology) | Self-actualization (Psychology) | Christian life. | LCGFT: Biographies. | Autobiographies. | BISAC: SPORTS & RECREATION / Coaching / Psychology. | SELF-HELP / Personal Growth / Success. | RELIGION / Christian Living / Personal Growth.
Classification: LCC: GV706.4 .V46 2026 | DDC: 796.01--dc23

Ordering Information: Special discounts are available on quantity purchases by corporations, associations, athletic organizations, and others. For details, contact us at: mike@mikevanhoozer.com.

Limit of Liability/Disclaimer of Warranty: The advice and strategies contained herein may not be suitable for your situation. You should consult with a professional where appropriate. Neither the publisher nor the author shall be liable for any loss of profit or any other commercial damages, including but not limited to special, incidental, consequential, or other damages.

Scripture Quotations: Unless otherwise noted, Scripture quotations marked (NIV) are taken from the Holy Bible, New International Version®, NIV®. Copyright © 1973, 1978, 1984, 2011 by Biblica, Inc.™ Used by permission. All rights reserved worldwide. Scripture quotations marked ESV are from the ESV Bible © (The Holy Bible, English Standard Version), copyright © 2001 by Crossway, a publishing ministry of Good News Publishers. Used by permission. All rights reserved. Scripture quotations marked NASB are from the New American Standard Bible © (NASB), copyright © 1960, 1971, 1977, 1995, 2020 by The Lockman Foundation, Used by permission. All rights reserved.

Cover and Interior Book Design: Amanda Blake Design

Contents

To Janell,
Thanks for allowing me to be a part of your journey!
For His Glory,
Mike

Introduction

SEAN CURRAN, "ALL PRAISE"

She was a friend you could always count on. A person you could trust. A leader you would follow. A follower of Jesus. And she played the game of golf. She played so well that she earned some incredible achievements in her golfing career.

But she was much more than just an incredible golfer, and that's what true greatness is all about – significance beyond your sport or platform. True greatness focuses on being the best person you can be and achieving your personal best in order to inspire others to become their best... and that is what Janell's life was all about...selfless exceptionalism.

In his book *greatness*, my friend, mentor, and sports psychologist and peak performance coach Dr. David Cook says: "Greatness is defined as selfless exceptionalism. Choosing a selfless heart is the defining pillar of greatness. It is a place of exceptional performances for the purpose of enhancing and encouraging the lives of others. When you choose greatness, you perform to inspire and encourage, you lead to inspire and encourage, your life mission is to make the lives of those around you—your team, community, nation, and world—better during the journey."[2]

Janell Marie Lysack Joslin personified David's definition of greatness. And she truly lived out Proverbs 4:26 (ESV), which was her theme verse:

"Ponder the path of your feet;

then all your ways will be sure."

She pursued greatness on and off the course to inspire others. She maximized her talent to honor God and encouraged others to do the same. She wanted to make the world a better place by engaging fully in the life she had been given instead of just going through the motions and taking up space.

But how did she get here? Was she born like this? Was she always a leader? Did she have doubts? Did she ever struggle, and did she face setbacks along the way?

We can all learn something from her journey. This is why I wrote this book: to honor her life, to tell you about the journey of Janell, and share 5 key principles that she learned and mastered. These principles helped her faith overcome her fear, building resiliency and mental toughness as she gradually learned to apply them. It's a story worth telling, a life worth remembering, and an example worth following.

My father-in-law, Dr. Barry Landrum, was an incredible man, pastor, and communicator! He told funny stories and was once asked if the stories he told, especially about himself, were true. His response: "There are 3 kinds of stories that I tell. Stories that are true. Stories that are based on truth. And stories that just might happen."

This book is comprised of all 3 of these components. Janell's story is true and almost all of the events actually happened. Some parts have been added based on truth and conversations and moments that just might have happened although some of the names and exact dialogue were added.

This book is for:

- Athletes who are looking to discover their identity beyond the court, the course, or their respective field of play and want to play *from a place of acceptance* instead of *for acceptance.*
- Anyone who may be struggling with confidence, dealing with doubt, and overwhelmed by the weight of his or her anxiety.
- Leaders who want to learn how to lead well from a servant leader's heart.
- People who are haunted by the feeling that they could be better.
- Anyone who wants to perform at his or her best, build a "championship mindset," and become the person they were created to be.

If you identify with any of these personas, I invite you to read more about the journey of Janell. You will learn that you can play from acceptance instead of for acceptance. Doubt and anxiety don't have to have the final word. You can build a championship mindset and actually have a faith that overcomes your fears. You can maximize your leadership potential and impact.

In these pages, you will learn about a person who possessed *grit* – a will to compete – and *grace* – a discerning and compassionate spirit – and who learned some key principles along the path of her journey that took her "game" and her life to the next level.

The journey of Janell can help us understand our own journey and help us traverse this path called life with humility, purpose, confidence, character, and servant leadership.

CHAPTER 1
"Tell Us That Story"

"Tell us that story!"

"Which one?" Janell asked.

"You know which one!" said a group of 10-12 year old girls. "The one when you won the tournament and led your team to the State Tournament!"

This group of girls was not just any group. They were a special collection of aspiring female golfers. After college, Janell moved to Nashville and was serving as an Assistant Golf Pro at Hermitage Golf Course. She created this program to help teach the game of golf to young girls. Along the way, they came to be known as "JJ's Juniors," named by the Hermitage Golf Course members who would see a circle of young golfers following their noble leader around the course.

Janell saw herself in the eyes of these girls. Eventually, the boys who played at the club also joined JJ's Juniors because they did not want to miss out on learning from the new golf coach.

She thought back to all of the sports she had participated in during her elementary and junior high school years and all of the lessons that sports had taught her. She also remembered the moment when she decided to solely focus on golf, a game that places all of the responsibility on the individual. Janell taught these young golfers the game of golf and showed them how lessons learned on the links translate to wisdom for life both now and in the future.

As Janell prepared to tell this group of young golfers her story, she remembered a coffee shop conversation with Mike, her mental performance coach, as they were preparing for a collegiate tournament.

"You're going to be a great instructor someday!" Mike boldly predicted.

"I don't even know what I want to do when I graduate from college," Janell responded.

"Well, I know that golf will be a part of you whatever you decide. You will not only be able to teach people how to play technically, but you will also be able to help them develop their mental game. That's a great combination and the best kind of golf teacher a person could ever ask for."

Mike was in full prophecy and hype mode, as Janell laughed, but she also thought about his words in that moment and wondered: "Would this be in her future? Was teaching golf what God was calling her to do? And how would it happen?"

Janell refocused on the current moment and as the girls excitedly began to ask her even more loudly to tell the story, she decided how to answer.

"Come on, JJ! Tell us! Tell us how you beat the other golfers! We want to know the secret to your success?"

"Okay! Okay! I will tell you the story...*again*! But you have to sit down, because I can't just tell you how it ends. We must start at the beginning. You see, a wise person once told me that it's the process that helps you become who God created you to be. You must enjoy the journey and embrace the moments along the way."

CHAPTER 2
The Meeting

"If you don't remember someone out loud, they die twice."
– MILES, EQUALIZER 2

She didn't want to meet with him.

"Mom, do I have to meet with this guy?" Janell asked in a frustrated tone. "What are we even going to talk about? Who is he again?"

These are normal questions for a high school student getting ready to meet with a *mental performance coach.*

Janell tried again. "Mom, please let me just go hit some more reps on the range."

After patiently enduring Janell's attempts to get out of the meeting, her mom said, "Just meet with him once. One time is all I ask. If you don't like it, you don't have to meet with him again."

Janell considered the proposition from her mom and consented to the ONE meeting. She had a very good relationship with her mom and knew she typically recommended what was in her best interest. I mean how bad could it be? At least she was getting free Starbucks!

As Janell thought about this upcoming meeting, she wondered, "What would he say? What questions would he ask me? Could he possibly help me? And what help did I really need? I mean, I only missed a putt at the biggest tournament of the year. It was just one putt. My game will get back on track...eventually."

Yet, that putt was still haunting her as she lamented the lost opportunity to win a medal at the state tournament, and she worried:

What if she could never let go of the past? What if she felt the weight of pressure in another big moment and missed a putt...again? What if this "valley moment" would haunt her for the rest of her life sabotaging her attempts in present and future moments to win and be successful?

The day arrived for her to meet with "the guy." It had been a busy week of practice, and she had not thought much again about the meeting. It was just one more thing on her schedule. An appointment that she could attend, check off the list, and then move on to getting back on the course. Her mom asked for one meeting and that it was all that she had planned on. One meeting. Yet, little did she know that her agreement to free Starbucks would be a pivotal point in her life and be something she would never forget. One moment in time to change the trajectory of her life.

As she walked into Starbucks, she looked around to see if there was anyone looking to meet with someone. As she scanned the coffee shop, she saw a man sitting in the corner near the door. He immediately got up and introduced himself.

"Hello Janell! I'm Mike," the man said in a friendly and welcoming voice. "Do you want to get some coffee?"

Janell processed his words and said, "Sure."

"What is your favorite?" he asked.

"Favorite?" Janell asked in a puzzled voice.

"Favorite coffee drink," he explained.

"Oh, I usually get a Vanilla Bean Frappuccino."

"Ok, sounds great! I already got a Mocha, and I have a table for us over here. You can put your stuff down, get your drink, and we can get started."

Janell ordered her favorite Frappuccino and joined Mike at the corner table. She wondered as she sat down if she would see anyone she knew, but her mind quickly went to what this meeting would be about.

"How has your day been?" he asked inquisitively.

Janell responded, "It has been great. I hit some golf balls at the range, worked on some putting, and am now meeting with you. I may go back to the course for some more practice later."

"That sounds great," Mike replied. "Let's get started. What did your mom tell you about me and about this meeting?"

"She said you work with athletes on their mental game."

"That's right," Mike confirmed. "I have had the honor of working with a lot of athletes at the high school, college, and professional level helping them maximize their potential and achieve their goals, including golfers such as yourself. The mental game is an 'X-factor,' or a key ingredient, that can help you both on and off the course. It can separate you from your competition. And it is something that can be developed and improved."

Mike explained how he got into sports psychology, how he met his mentor David Cook, and how David encouraged him to make this a part of what he was doing.

As Mike continued to talk, Janell began to see this moment as more than just a meeting. She did not know what the future would hold or if she would meet with Mike again, but she began to engage in the conversation and open herself up to the possibility of something good coming from this encounter.

Janell answered questions about her family, her past performances, her strengths as a golfer and as a person. Mike also asked her to rate herself on a scale of 1-10 on how she felt about herself as a golfer and as a person. She had never really been asked this question, and she paused to consider her answer.

The last several months had been interesting, and she had experienced a whirlwind of emotions. The thrill of a successful spring season and sophomore year. The mix of tournament wins and accomplishments, including winning her second District MVP Award and being selected captain of the golf team again. The ascent through the district and region tournament. And the missed putt that dropped her out of a medal spot at the State tournament that led to this meeting. The missed putt was why she was here in this moment meeting with a mental performance coach.

Sports, like life, are filled with highs and lows. Wins and losses. Successes and setbacks. Mountaintop moments and valley moments. The tendency is often to remember the disappointing times and forget the incredible achievements, never realizing that you need to do the opposite. A championship mindset is built upon choosing to focus on positive and productive thoughts that will help you navigate the highs and lows and twists and turns of your journey.

Janell thought for another moment and then said, "6! I feel like a 6 as a golfer."

"And as a person?" Mike asked.

"9!" Janell answered. "I feel like a 9 as a person."

"Ok, great!" Mike responded. "Help me understand why you chose those 2 numbers to rate your feelings about the two roles."

Janell answered, "I chose 6 as a golfer because while I know I have the God-given talent to play golf and have achieved a lot over this past year, I have had trouble rebounding and getting back into a groove since the state tournament."

"Tell me about the state tournament. What happened that caused you to feel this way about your golf game? What caused you to get off course?"

While Mike knew what happened from Janell's mom during the phone call to arrange this meeting, he wanted to hear Janell tell the story in her own words.

"I missed a 4-foot putt. A putt I should have made, and it caused me to drop down in the final tournament standings. It was the difference between earning a medal and missing a moment. I know life is not all about awards and medals, but I wanted this one! And I thought I should have achieved it, and it didn't happen. If I am being honest, I am still disappointed."

"I understand," Mike replied. "I know that must have hurt when it happened. Tell me about your other rating. You gave yourself a rating of 9 as a person. Tell me about that number."

"I gave myself a 9 because I feel good about myself as a person – both who I am and who I am becoming," Janell answered as her mood became slightly more positive.

When you move past moments of anguish and regain perspective about your identity, including who you are and the opportunities you have, it opens your mind to a broader and better perspective. You understand that you have a choice and an opportunity to zoom out of the micro-moment of pain and focus on the macro-moment of purpose.

"That's great," Mike affirmed. "You know your identity is not tied to your performance. You realize it is much broader than just being a golfer. What you do is not who you are."

Janell reflected on his words including that last declaration, and she personalized it in her mind:

What I do is not who I am

She knew this statement was true, but for so long, she had tied her identity to what she did. And what she did most of the time was play golf. Of course, people knew her as Janell, but they also knew her as a golfer. She reflected on how so much of her identity was based on how she performed. This was true for her and for her peers who played sports. She knew she did not have to base the essence of who she was on a golf score, but she would need some tools and new thought processes to help make this truth become a reality in her life.

"Now, I am going to draw something," Mike said as he took a notebook and a pen out of his backpack. "My wife is an art teacher and a very talented artist. I am not a very good artist, but I think you will get the point of this picture. This is what we call the I-R Model," he said as he drew the letter I and a bunch of Rs around the I, almost like planets orbiting around a center of the universe.

"We call it the I-R Model because it has an 'I' and a lot of 'Rs' on it. 'I' stands for Identity, and 'R' stands for Role. The 'I' represents you. Your gifts. Your talents. How you are wired. How God created you to be uniquely you. And 'R' represents the roles you play in life. You are a daughter. A sister. A student. A golfer. A friend. A leader. And you probably play many other roles."

THE IDENTITY ROLE MODEL

I=Identity | R=Role

"The Identity-Role model can help explain why your performance spirals downward when you base your identity on your performance. For example, you rated yourself as a 6 in your sport and a 9 for your identity as a person. A lower role-based rating in one area of your life can tend to bring down the rating that you gave yourself as a person, negatively affecting how you feel about other roles in your life.

"When it comes to confidence, many people derive their confidence based on external circumstances or outcomes. I call this an 'outside-in' approach to confidence, and I believe this is the wrong way to achieve and maintain confidence in your life. It sounds something like this: 'If

I play well today, I will feel good about myself,' or 'If I make this putt, I will feel good about myself.' Janell, have you ever felt this way, and can you relate to this method of trying to build confidence?"

"Yes, I have definitely done that before!" Janell answered. She thought this was the way every athlete in any sport claimed confidence. Confidence comes from results, or so she thought it should.

"At the end of the day, every athlete is judged by a metric, a score, a time, and an outcome," Mike continued. "It is only natural to feel good about yourself when you achieve that outcome and to feel bad when you don't. The biggest issue is when you tie your performance – a thing you do not have full control over – straight to your identity, or who you are as a person and your self-worth.

"This outside-in approach to confidence, identity, and self worth is based on results, outcomes, and things you can influence but not control," Mike continued to explain. "When you put your faith and identity in things you cannot control, you become disappointed and desperate when the outcome doesn't meet your expectation. Your identity takes a hit, and you wonder if you have what it takes to succeed. When you do this, you are living out of this 'math' equation:

Identity = Performance + Opinion of Others

"Operating out of this equation looks like this:
- Did I play well?
- Did my coach/parents/peers say I did well?
- Then, I feel good about myself and my identity.
OR...

- Did I play badly?
- Did my coach/parents/peers say I did bad, or did I perceive or feel that they did not think I played well?
- Then, I feel bad about myself and my identity.

"I believe that this equation and the outside-in approach to confidence is not the way to perform at your best. Fortunately for you, there is another way. A better way."

Janell was intrigued with this new model and could definitely relate to how old models of thinking could get in the way of her performing at her best. She wanted a better way and was excited to hear about it.

"As you look at the I-R Model again, think about what it would look like for you to step onto the golf course and be confident, courageous, focused, and at peace with whatever may happen. I believe this is possible based on how you use the Performance equation and how you derive your confidence.

"I think you can understand that the Outside-In approach to confidence does not work, especially on a long-term, consistent basis. The Inside-Out approach to confidence, however, does work, and I have used it with countless athletes across all sports and performance areas to help people perform consistently at their best. The key is to shift your mindset to trust all of the things that you have done to prepare for this moment:

- Your hard work
- Your past successes
- Your perseverance through setbacks
- The positive feedback from coaches, parents, teammates, and peers
- Your purposeful preparation for tournaments

"Janell, your mind is like a DVR, and you control the things that you replay. It is a different mindset when instead of basing your confidence on a condition ('If I play well'), you base your confidence on things you can control like your preparation and hard work. You begin to say things like:

"I feel good about myself today based on the preparation and hard work that I have done. Regardless of the results, I will feel good about who I am and what I am capable of accomplishing."

"When you think like this, you are basing your confidence on things you can control which ultimately affects and influences things you cannot control but can influence like your results.

"Peak performers who utilize the 'Inside-Out' approach to confidence live out of a different 'math' equation:

Performance = Talent - Distractions.

"Instead of tying your performance to your identity, the best performers in sports, business, and life look at each of their roles in life and seek to do their best based on the talent and opportunities they have been given. They use this equation to maximize their talent and minimize the distractions that keep them from performing well. Maximizing talent involves process-oriented things like:

- A great pre-shot routine
- A consistent pre-game or pre-performance routine that you believe in and that keeps you focused, peaceful, and present
- Playing to your strengths

"Minimizing distractions involves using tips and techniques to avoid the things that get in the way of your performance, many of which you cannot control. Distractions involve things like:

- The weather
- The talent of another golfer
- Things that other golfers say or do
- Past performances

"Janell, what are some other distractions that get in the way of performing at your best in golf?" Mike asked.

"A missed putt. The design of the golf course. Water. Sand. Thinking about what other golfers are shooting that day," Janell answered as she thought about how quickly she came up with this list and how often she thought about these things.

"That's right," Mike confirmed. "There are a lot of things that can distract us and get in the way of our best performances if we let them. But we don't have to do that. We don't have to let distractions detour us from our path to peak performance. Do you want to know how?"

"Yes, I do," Janell answered.

And then Mike asked a weird question. "Janell, have you ever been swimming in a pool?"

"Yes," she answered with a puzzled look on her face, wondering where this part of the conversation was going and what in the world it had to do with golf.

Mike continued, "If you have ever been around a lake, pool, or body of water, you have probably seen a beach ball and know what happens when you try and push a beach ball underneath the water. It pops up out of the water! And when someone tries even harder to get the beach ball further underneath the water by sitting on it, the ball shoots up out of the water even stronger and higher and the person sitting on the beach ball falls over. The same is true when you try and press or repress – press over and over – the five forces in your mind.

"In competition, it is always important to know your opponent. Notice, I did not say fear your opponent. Knowing your opponent involves understanding what you are up against in order for you to design the right strategy to overtake the competition.

"There are five forces that rise up against you on an individual level to keep you from performing at your best," Mike further explained. "Unlike an individual opponent, these five forces attack you from within. They wage a mental battle that can be more debilitating than any external force. Every time you toe the line, attempt a shot, throw a pass or pitch, step up to the plate, or step over your golf ball, they heckle you. They falsely proclaim lies. They tell you that you're not good enough. That you are worthless and don't have what it takes. Before you ever face a competitor, you must learn to conquer these mental forces in order to show up on game day ready, focused, and confident. The Five Forces are:

- Fear
- Pressure
- Doubt
- Negative Thoughts
- Lack of Confidence

"When a negative thought like 'What if I miss?' or 'What if I fail?' pops in your head, repeatedly saying things like 'Don't think about it!' does not work to erase these thoughts. That response is like trying to press, or repress, the beach ball underneath the water. The negative thought, fear, doubt, or other destructive force is going to come back up in your mind stronger and more forceful."

Janell thought about these forces and wondered if she had let them deter her from playing her best golf. While she did not think dealing with pressure or fear were issues for her, she remembered instances when negative thoughts distracted her, which surprised her because she was a very positive and optimistic person. She also could relate to having doubt while standing over a shot or putt, which prevented her from playing her best golf and fully unleashing her talent. Janell recognized how doubt sometimes had shaken her confidence.

"Janell, you have to **_replace, not repress_** the negative forces of fear, pressure, doubt, lack of confidence, and negative thoughts with what we call a trigger, or activating, phrase. A trigger phrase is defined as a 2-3 word phrase that triggers or activates something physically for you. It needs to be a phrase that communicates trust and belief and is tied to the physical actions related to your sport that result in success. For example, if you suddenly have a thought like 'What if I hit it in the water?', you can replace that thought with a phrase like 'Trust My Shot!' A baseball player who fears 'What if I strike out?' can use a trigger phrase of 'Stay back,' to keep his weight back which will trigger the right stance, mindset, and approach to simplifying the hitting process.

"A good trigger/activating phrase:

- Is 2-3 words in length
- Uses the format Verb-Object
- Is tied to physical cues related to your sport
- Encourages trust and belief
- Means something powerful to you and should activate a positive physical response from you
- Stays fixed in your mind, allowing you to be focused and present in the moment

Mike then continued to explain about the power of words and phrases and how your self-talk affects your mindset, which affects your actions. He spoke with passion about how words and mindset have power to help you achieve greatness or to hinder you from becoming your best. The final lesson focused on why an activating phrase could have power in a tournament round of golf.

"What you think about can and will affect your outcomes," Mike explained. "In other words, if you are thinking about water when you step up to a hit a tee shot on the golf course or about failing in some way, you are more likely to experience the setback you fear the most. If you are thinking positive thoughts about hitting your target or succeeding in some way, you are more likely to accomplish that goal. The mere presence of a negative or positive thought does not guarantee the outcome, but your body will follow what your mind is focused on. For this reason, you need to be focused on positive and productive phrases that can replace the negative thoughts of fear and doubt."

Janell suddenly had an epiphany, and she realized that these principles were not just about golf. They were principles that were applicable in any area of her life. She also realized that this meeting was a defining moment that all began with a missed putt!

Mike closed out the meeting by telling Janell, "There is a lot more to learn and more that I want to share with you, but it is up to you if you want to continue these coaching sessions. I wanted to make sure you received value from this coaching session, which can serve as a catalyst for future moments. Talk with your parents and let me know."

"Thanks so much, and it was great meeting you!" Janell replied as they left the coffee shop.

Janell's mom was there to pick her up but delayed asking her anything about the meeting.

As they pulled up in the driveway, Janell said, "I'm really glad you encouraged me to meet with him. I think he can help me, and I want to meet with him again."

CHAPTER 3

Developing a Championship Mindset

"Well, she wants to meet with you again," Janell's mom, Donna, said on a phone call to check in with Mike. "I don't know what you said or what you talked about, but it must have been good, because it clicked with Janell."

"That's great, and I am so glad it was a good meeting for her," Mike responded.

"Janell has so much potential!" Donna responded. "She's a special leader and a true light to her friends. We just want to support her in this journey to help her become the best she can be."

"Well, I am glad to help in any way I can," Mike said. "When can she meet again?"

"Let me check with her and her schedule, and we will let you know," Donna answered. "Thanks so much!"

Later that day, Mike got a text message from Janell's mom confirming that Janell could meet next week.

The days had flown by as Janell reviewed some of the things that she had learned from her first coaching session with Mike. She began to apply some of the principles and techniques they discussed both in practices and in a couple of tournaments. There were moments of success and moments of learning. She was on the right path; she just wished the journey was more straightforward.

Janell entered the coffee shop, and Mike was waiting for her. They ordered and then sat down to continue what would become a 6-year coaching journey, though neither of them knew then the extent of how long it would last or what they would discover along the way.

"How are you doing?" Mike asked.

"I'm doing well! How are you?" Janell responded.

"I am doing great! Tell me about your last tournament. How did it go?"

"I did pretty good. There were definitely moments where I could have done better. I had some really good holes that were leading me to a great score and finish, but I had 2 holes that kept me from winning the tournament," Janell explained.

"That's how the game of golf sometimes plays out. It's the one or two holes or the one or two moments that make the difference between good and great. Between wins and defeat," Mike confirmed.

"And I felt so great walking out of the meeting with you the other day and was so excited to put it all together and go win this tournament!" Janell continued.

"I know, and that's great! I love that our coaching session resonated with you, and I appreciate your determined spirit. Remember, Janell, it's a process." Mike said.

"I know. I know. That's what you said the other day," Janell said somewhat reluctantly.

"And I will keep saying it, and you will keep growing and getting better because of what the process produces," Mike reassured her.

"So, what are we learning today?" Janell asked.

"Can you remember 5 things?"

"Yes, I can remember 5 things," Janell said with a smile and a hint of sarcasm.

"I want to share with you these 5 keys which will serve not only as a playbook for your mental game in golf but also as a playbook for life. I call them the *5 Keys to a Championship Mindset*. These 5 keys will help you develop mental toughness, build resiliency when things get challenging, and have faith over fear in any moment."

Mike paused not only to gather his thoughts but also to let the significance and weight of his words sink in. A playbook for golf. A playbook for life. The things he would share with Janell were simple, yet profound. Easy to understand, yet sometimes difficult to apply consistently in every moment.

"The first key is: *Play From a Place of Acceptance.*"

KEY 1
Play From a Place of Acceptance

Key Word: *Identity*

Janell immediately zeroed in on the word "acceptance." Throughout junior high and now high school, she had often seen her friends and peers yearn for acceptance. They would do almost anything to be accepted. By other students. By their coaches. By their parents. In dating relationships. And especially online through social media. She and her friends were navigating a world where they were judged by what they did versus accepted for who they were.

Janell also wondered if she had ever "played for acceptance." Were there moments and tournaments in the past where she had played to impress a college coach or for the approval of the people she was competing against?

Sensing that this first key resonated with her, Mike asked Janell, "Have you ever played for acceptance? And you can substitute the words confidence, validation, worth, and/or identity for the word 'acceptance.'"

Janell sighed, "Yes."

"Tell me more about that. What did playing *for acceptance* look like for you in that moment?"

"I can remember a few tournaments where I tried to prove myself to people who were watching me play," Janell explained. "Instead of playing free, I tried to force things to happen, and it did not work out for me. I tried to control the outcome, and the result was not good!"

"Yes, control is what we often want, but we will get to that word later," Mike said. "What about the idea of validation, worth, and acceptance? When you think about those words and the game that you play, what jumps out at you?"

"Well, I play a game that is based on a score, and the lowest score wins. I play a game where you are measured by that number."

"Do you ever judge your worth based on the number on your score-card?" Mike asked inquisitively already knowing what the answer would be based on the plethora of conversations he had been involved in with athletes across all sports.

"Yes, I have had moments when I judge myself based on what I shot on the golf course."

"And why is that?" Mike asked wanting her to think deeper.

"I spend a lot of time practicing. My parents invest a lot of money for lessons and tournaments supporting me in this sport. The girls I compete against want to beat me. And the friends I have outside of golf wonder why I can't hang out all the time. And most of all, I want to prove that I am a great golfer and that all of this hard work is worth it and is helping me accomplish my goals. For all of these reasons, I want to win the tournaments that I play in. And yes, I do sometimes compare myself to others and judge myself by a golf score."

Janell realized that she had never really verbalized these thoughts and emotions before. Had she been repressing them? Were these emotions that were just rising up in the moment, or were they more indicative of feelings that she needed to process and learn how to deal with?

"That's incredibly insightful!" Mike responded. "Do you remember the I-R Model we discussed in our first meeting?"

"Yes, I remember it. Is that part of the 5 things I need to remember?" Janell asked with a grin.

"It's connected to it," Mike said, amused by her wit. "When you judge yourself by a score and play for confidence from an outside-in approach motivated by external factors that you cannot control, you are playing 'for acceptance.'"

"So, what's the answer? How should I play?" Janell replied.

"As we discussed in our first coaching session, you have to play using an inside-out approach to confidence. You must play with a 'Because-of' mindset," Mike responded.

"What does that mean – a 'Because-of' mindset?" Janell asked.

"It means not basing your confidence, and, ultimately, your worth, validation, acceptance, and identity on whether you sink a putt or make a certain score. Instead, you step onto the course with confidence, knowing you have put in the work to play your best. It means that you don't tie your identity to your performance; you anchor and connect it to something more lasting and eternal. You play from an inner confidence because of your work, your practice, your support system, and your faith. Just to name a few things that you have in common with many other athletes that I have worked with that have created their Because-of truths."

"Interesting. I have often based my confidence on whether that first tee shot goes in the fairway or my first couple of holes lead to birdies. I know that my mindset won't shift just because you tell me to do this. How do I learn to play from a Because-Of mindset? How do I stop playing *for acceptance* and more consistently play *from a place of acceptance*?"

"Well, it's a process, Janell."

"You say that about everything! 'It's a process,'" Janell said with false frustration and a laugh repeating what Mike had repeatedly reiterated to her. "But I know what you are saying is right, and I want to invest in that process to grow and become better."

As the time came for them to end this coaching session, Mike said one more thing that Janell would embrace for the rest of her life.

"Janell, your life should never be defined by a metric. When all is said and done and you are standing before God, the question will be:

Did you accomplish the mission? Did you become who God created you to be and shine the light of Jesus through your life to a world that desperately needs Him?"

Janell left the coffee shop thinking about the conversation. She wondered: "Am I tying my identity to the wrong things? Is my acceptance anchored to the outcome of a shot? If I am being honest with myself, am I am basing my worth on a number on a scorecard and whether I won the day...or not?"

She began to journal some answers to questions that Mike had given her that looked like this:

PLAY FROM A PLACE OF ACCEPTANCE

- Where does your confidence come from?

- What are you tying your identity to?

- Who or what do you put your trust in?

- Develop 3 "Because of" statements.

After she finished, she read a few Bible verses, prayed, and went to sleep.

CHAPTER 4

Focus on What You Can Control

Another week went by. Practices. Planning for tournaments. Time with family and time with friends. It had been a typical summer in many ways, but Janell felt a shift happening. These meetings with her new mental coach seemed like a gift from God, and she was soaking in all that she could learn to become her best.

She also felt a need to share these lessons with others. Janell had always been a great leader amongst her peers, but not in a bossy kind of way. People loved hanging out with her, and she seemed to be everyone's best friend. She breathed life into others just by her presence. She encouraged others, saw the best in them, and helped them see the best in themselves. She focused on doing things with excellence and always for the glory of God.

She woke up and headed to the course to get in some practice and then went straight to Starbucks to meet with Mike. As she left the course, she wondered what they would be talking about today. As she walked through the door, Mike was there in the usual spot – a table tucked away in the corner by the window.

"Hello, Janell! How are you doing?" Mike said with an enthusiasm that seemed like he had already had enough espresso for the day. "How is your day going?"

"I am doing great!" Janell replied trying to match his enthusiasm. "I just came from the course after a very good round of practice."

"Are you getting your usual?" Mike asked.

"Yes...the usual," Janell said as she made her way to order a Vanilla Bean Frappucino.

As she sat down at the table, Janell asked Mike what the lesson for today would be. Mike told her that they would be covering the issue of control – a struggle for many of the athletes he worked with.

"When I say the word control, what comes to your mind?" Mike asked.

"Something I wish I had more of," she said.

"Most of us do! What I have found is that we often stress over the things we cannot control and invest less time in the things we can control. We try to control outcomes and situations. We try to control other people. We try to control circumstances. All of these are things we mistakenly think we can control, and then we wonder why we are stressed out.

"What are some things that you try to control?" Mike asked.

"I try to control my shots and where they go as well as outcomes and my score on specific holes or for the whole round," Janell responded.

"And do you ever get distracted or even frustrated by things you cannot control? And what are some examples of that?"

"I play an outdoor sport, so obviously the weather, but also hole design and pin placement can be a distraction."

"Yes, I mean golf course designers try to get you to focus on the trees, water, and sand versus the fairway, the green, and your target," Mike said agreeing with Janell's assessment.

"Yes, I mean I never thought about it what way. You're exactly right. It's almost like there is an enemy who doesn't want me to focus on the target and is working against me to worry about the distractions. I think distractions can steer us off course not only in golf but also in life," Janell responded thinking deeper about where this conversation was going and the impact it was going to have on how she lived her life.

"You're exactly right, Janell! There are a lot of things that we are going to discuss that transcend the golf course and are applicable to all aspects of life. Yes, these principles and keys to a championship mindset apply to sports and golf and can help you play your best. They will also help you become the person God created you to be amidst the distractions and storms of daily life. We have not talked about faith. Is faith important to you?"

Janell thoughtfully replied, "Yes, faith is important to me. I'm a Christian."

"So am I," Mike answered. "The Bible talks about fear and having faith over fear a lot. In fact, Jesus warns us about an enemy, or thief, who comes to steal, kill, and destroy in John 10:10. I often say that we have an enemy who comes to steal *our joy*, kill *our purpose*, and destroy *our impact*. We cannot take our focus off what we are doing on the golf course and even more so in life. Focusing on what you can control is the key."

"Sometimes I can get distracted, and, if I am being honest, even a little discouraged," Janell revealed. "My mind wanders to either past shots or future holes, and my focus strays from my current shot. I also sometimes allow the design of the course or the people I am competing against to get in my head. How do I stop worrying about things I can't control?"

Mike reflected on the question. He had heard so many athletes utter this phrase or some variation of it. Sometimes, it was phrased as a question with a yearning to find an answer: "How do I get out of my own head or way and play my best?" Other times, it was a statement or even a declaration: "I can't get out of my head!"

Mike responded to Janell, "The second key is: ***Focus on What You Can Control.***"

KEY 2
Focus on What You Can Control

Key Word: *Focus*

"There are two axioms, or principles, that I use related to this second key that can make a big difference in the way you look at situations and learn to focus on what you can control."

He then tore a page out of his notebook and said as he wrote the first principle:

What You Choose to Focus on Magnifies in Size

He let the idea sink in and then said it again, only this time he emphasized the third word: "*choose*."

"Janell, every word is important in this phrase. It's not what we focus on that magnifies in size. It's what we *choose* to focus on that magnifies in size," Mike explained.

"So, what you're saying is that my choices matter," Janell responded with a smile that showed she got the point he was making. She appreciated his style of making the point crystal clear so she did not miss it.

"Yes! Your choices matter! In golf and in life. In what club you choose and in what friends you choose. Choices matter, and what you choose to focus on magnifies in size. In golf, if you choose to focus on or worry about the sand, trees, or water on a hole, then these distractions become bigger and bigger in your mind. If you choose to focus on your target, then it will become bigger and bigger, magnifying in size in your mind. What you focus on is your choice, so choose wisely. Choose to focus on positive and productive thoughts that will position you for success."

"Wow, I never thought it about that way, and that makes a lot of sense! I can't let errant thoughts and distractions get in the way of playing my best. I have the freedom to choose what thoughts I allow to linger in my mind, which ones I want to magnify, and which ones I want to minimize. I can also focus on the things that are within my control like my energy, my effort, my attitude, and my self-talk. I think I got the first 'axiom.' Isn't that what you called it?" Janell asked with a wry smile acting like she had never heard that word before and also throwing some good-natured shade at Mike for the use of the vocabulary word of the day.

Janell continued, "I think you said there were 2 axioms, or principles, connected to the second key to a championship mindset of Focus on What You Can Control. What is the second phrase I need to learn?"

"The second 'axiom' is:

Every Action Begins With a Thought

"Everything you do on the golf course and in life begins with a thought. Before you take a swing and before you say a word, you will have at least one if not many thoughts going through your mind. So, the key question is: What thoughts are you thinking? The good news is you have the power to choose. Janell, what do you think about before you take a swing?"

Janell responded, "Sometimes, I think and even say out loud, 'What if I hit this shot in the water?' Or 'What if I don't make this putt?' 'What if I don't win this tournament?'"

"And do those thoughts help you or hinder you?" Mike asked.

"They hinder me!" Janell uttered without hesitation. "And they usually lead to bad shots and unintended consequences like hitting the shot exactly where I was trying to avoid hitting it. Negative thoughts prevent me from playing at my best."

"That's right. Focusing on the right thoughts is one of the most important parts of the process in order to hit a great shot and, ultimately, achieve a great score. You must think about what you think about and make adjustments as necessary. This process is called a *thought audit*," Mike said.

"What's a thought audit?" Janell asked curiously.

"A thought audit is a process where you evaluate your thoughts, much like an accountant performs an *audit* of a company's financials to make sure they are valid and true. A mental evaluation of your thoughts can include questions like 'Is this thought true?' and 'Is it helpful?' I usually have my athletes debrief their practices and performances and evaluate if any negative thoughts have been entering their mind and their self-talk. For example, sometimes I will have an athlete who tells me the following:

"Tomorrow I am just going to worry about this."

"What is wrong with that statement?" Mike asked, wanting Janell to learn this new process for herself.

"They used the word 'worry.' They said they were going to worry about something," Janell replied, knowing that she had probably allowed that little phrase to slide into her self-talk as well.

"That's right!" Mike confirmed. "They said they were going to worry about it. Now, I know what they were intending to say, but what would have been a better thought and word choice?"

Janell's answer sounded like a question, "Focus?"

"That's correct," Mike affirmed. "Focus is a better word than worry. Instead of saying 'Tomorrow, I am going to worry about that,' they could change the phrase to say, 'Tomorrow, I am going to focus on this!' That simple word change can make a tremendous difference in the way we process our thoughts and emotions and how we perform in competition and show up in life!"

Your thoughts are vital to your mental health. Craig Groeschel says, "Our lives are always moving in the direction of our strongest thoughts. What we think shapes who we are."[1] So, if your thoughts are always shaping who you are, who you are becoming, and the direction of your life, you can't be casual in your approach to what and how you think.

You must be purposeful and intentional, and you must evaluate and process your thoughts.

Janell was learning that the battle for your mind is real. She was realizing that there was a "spiritual enemy" who wanted her and everyone else to believe lies instead of truths and to focus on words and phrases that were limiting beliefs. While Janell was an optimistic person, she knew that she needed to constantly guard her heart and mind.

She knew she needed to replace limiting beliefs that would sometimes slip into her thoughts and self-talk with liberating truths and conquering beliefs that would help her develop a championship mindset.

"And that brings us to the end of our coaching session and to your next homework assignment. It's not a hard assignment, and I am not trying to add to the list of things you have to do. I don't want to be the guy who gives you homework during the summer! I want you to do 2 things. First, make a list of all of the things that are within your control and another list of things that are outside of your control. For the list of things that are outside of your control, I want you to take a look at it and then crumple it up and throw it away vowing never to worry or spend time thinking about those things again.

"For the list of the things that are within your control, I want you to keep it in a prominent place. Take a screenshot of it and review it often on your phone. Type it again in your favorite notes app on your phone. Reflect on the things that you place on this list – the factors that are within your sphere of influence and control – and commit to focusing on these things consistently and often.

"The second assignment is to perform a thought audit. I want you to think about any words that you currently say or that find their way into your self-talk as you go about your day and especially on the golf course that are not helpful, positive, or productive. Spend about a week analyzing, auditing, and looking for these destructive and distracting words and write them down in a single column on a piece of paper. Then, I want you to review the list and think of a better word for each word on the list. A word that is helpful, positive, and more productive. Feel free to send these two things to me for feedback. If you have questions, we can discuss it in our coaching session next week."

"Sounds great!" Janell responded.

As she walked out of the door of the coffee shop, Janell's mind started thinking about the assignments, and more importantly, everything that she and Mike had just discussed. She wondered how much mental and emotional energy she had been wasting on things outside of her control. What if she could make a shift – a shift in her mindset – and redirect her attention and focus to the things that matter most? What kind of impact would that have not only in golf, but also in life?

That night, Janell sat down on her bed and began to journal about her day, what she had observed, and what she had learned. She also reviewed the questions Mike had given her:

FOCUS ON WHAT
YOU CAN CONTROL

- What is in your control?

- What is out of your control?

- How can you work on better focusing your mind & attention on what you can control?

Since the assignments were fresh on her mind, she developed the two lists and performed the thought audit. This is what her lists looked like:

THINGS <u>OUTSIDE</u> OF MY CONTROL:

- The Weather
- The Design of the Golf Course
- The Layout of a Certain Hole
- How Others Perform
- The Opinions of Other People
- A Coach's Decision to Offer Me a College Scholarship

THINGS <u>WITHIN</u> MY CONTROL:

- My Attitude
- My Energy
- My Effort
- My Thoughts
- My Self-talk
- My Commitment to My Pre-Shot Routine
- Staying Focused on My Process
- How I Choose to Invest My Time
- How I Respond

MY THOUGHT AUDIT:

NEGATIVE THOUGHT	A BETTER THOUGHT
Worry	Focus
I'll Try	I Will
If	When
Control	Impact
My Worst	My Best

Janell looked at her list and reflected on what she was learning. She was discovering that these keys to a championship mindset that Mike was teaching her existed inside of her. She just needed a framework to help her fulfill her potential and someone to ask the right questions and share the right information and insight to unleash her talent.

She closed her journal, went to sleep, and dreamed of what God had in store for her.

Janell was a leader, and she was learning to become all God created her to be.

Lots of Questions

"Coach JJ! Coach JJ! We have questions! Lots of questions!" The girls exclaimed in unison like a choir or maybe more like journalists at a press conference with their favorite professional coach or athlete.

"Okay, let's go one at a time, and I will answer your questions. But let's don't shout them out. Remember, we are at a golf course, and we have to respect the other members and have proper etiquette. Raise your hand, and I will call on you," Janell said sensing their excitement.

She loved this group of girls. She remembered her younger years – hanging out at the golf course, practicing, working on her game, and playing the Texas Junior Golf Tour. She dreamed of these moments. She reflected on how when she was growing up, there were not many examples of female golfers. Most of her friends were either hanging out with their friends or playing sports like volleyball and soccer, so very few of her friends could help her navigate what it was like to be a young female on a golf course or at a country club. She wanted to help these young female golfers learn to play golf, to respect the game, and to be respected as leaders on and off the course.

"Reagan, you have your hand up. What's your question?"

"What does the word etiquette mean?" Reagan asked.

"I thought you had questions about my story – the one I was telling ya'll."

"We do, but you said we need to have proper etiquette, and we don't know what that means," Reagan responded persistently.

"Etiquette is your behavior. It means to respect and show consideration for others, especially in certain situations or places. And it could be different for different places. At a football game, you cheer...loudly... for the whole game. On the golf course, you don't shout and you remain quiet when other people are taking a shot. I am sure that your parents are teaching you proper manners like saying 'Yes, ma'am' and 'Yes, sir' and 'Please' and 'Thank You.' Manners are a part of proper etiquette."

"Ok, thanks. I have another question," Reagan continued.

"Is it about etiquette?" Janell asked with a smile.

"No, you explained that pretty well. It's about your story. You said that at the beginning, you did not want to meet with Coach Mike. Why didn't you want to meet with him?" Reagan asked curiously.

"That's a great question, Reagan. If I had known what was on the other side of meeting with Mike, I would never have begged my mom not to go, and I would have done it much sooner! I guess it had to do with going to see a mental performance coach. For most people, they don't want to admit that they need help. And I believe it's even worse for athletes who think they could do anything and everything on their own. And if someone suggests that they have an issue with their mind and need to go see someone, they see that as being weak.

"For me, I didn't know what we were going to talk about and thought I could just handle the issue myself by just getting back on the range and hitting more golf balls. I didn't know that working with someone on my mental game could be an X Factor and a positive for me. I mistakenly saw it as a negative and something only people with real mental health problems did as a last resort, not a first response."

"What's an X Factor?" Meredith chimed in.

"An X Factor, as defined by my mental performance coach, is something that separates you from the competition. When things like talent, strategy, and golf clubs and gear are equal to yours, a strong mental game can separate you from the person you are competing against. You are able to persevere and be resilient when other golfers want to quit and give up."

"Okay, thanks!" Meredith said.

"I have one more question," Reagan insisted.

"Wow, Reagan! You are very curious today. You can ask one more, and then I need to get back to telling the story to finish it before it gets dark and ya'll have to go home."

"When did you know you were a great golfer?"

This question seemed to linger and echo in the ears of Janell and the other junior golfers. The other girls turned quickly from Reagan to Coach JJ to see what she would say. They all wanted to know what it meant to be great.

And how do you know if and when you are great? And what does it mean to be great? There was so much depth and so many layers to this question that not even Reagan knew what she was really asking.

Janell thought about what Reagan was asking, paused, and then said, "Reagan, that is a profound question, and before you ask, profound means your question is deep, insightful, and thoughtful. There is a simple answer I could give you, but let's continue with the story. I think the more profound answer will be revealed to you by the time I finish. Any more questions, girls? Can we continue with the story that you asked, no, begged me to tell?"

"Yes!" the girls – JJ's Juniors – responded in an excited chorus.

"We always have questions – and lots of them – but we will wait until you finish the story to ask them," Meredith added.

"Sounds great! Now, where were we in the story? Oh yeah, I remember. I was talking about focusing on the process."

CHAPTER 5

Outcome-Driven and Process-Focused

"I learned that when you love the process, you will love what the process produces."
– JON GORDON, THE ONE TRUTH

Another week went by. Another practice. Another tournament. And another moment to shine, grow, learn, and compete. Janell was having an incredible summer. She remembered how she felt at the end of her golf season in the spring after soaring so high and having a letdown in a big moment at the State Tournament. While it had only been a couple of months, it felt like ages ago. She had a new outlook on golf and life. She was learning to not allow her identity to be defined by a golf score or a bad shot. She was also choosing better thoughts and demonstrating a laser focus on the things that she could control and influence. She was learning not to waste mental and emotional energy on things that she could not control.

It was Tuesday, and it had been a week since her last coaching session with Mike. She looked forward to telling him about the progress she was making not only in golf, but more specifically, in her mental game. She was ready to debrief the last tournament and also show him her homework assignment. As she walked into the coffee shop, Mike was waiting for her.

"Hi Janell. How are you?" Mike asked with a smile.

"I'm doing great! How are you?" Janell responded.

"Wow! I love the energy! Someone must be having a great week!"

"Someone is having a great week, and I hope yours has gone well too! I can't wait to tell you about my tournament and show you my homework assignment."

They both ordered and sat down at the table by the window, which always seemed to be available and waiting for a moment such as this.

"Did you do your homework?"

"I did!" Janell replied confidently.

"That's great! But first let's talk about your tournament. How did it go? What did you do well? And what did you learn?"

Janell noticed that Mike seemed to always ask the same questions whenever he wanted to debrief a tournament. And he never began with "What score did you shoot?" It seemed like he was more concerned with how she felt about the round. And she thought the other two questions were interesting as well. "What did I do well? And what did I learn?"

She had never had a coach ask her these questions, especially a question about learning from a tournament. If anything, the questions often centered around the things that she didn't do well. She would occasionally think about that in her own self-assessment. Before she began meeting with Mike, she would think about one or two things that she did well and then lament the longer list of things that she didn't do well.

Mike could tell that she was considering what he just asked so he provided some additional context and a little bit of filler time for her to thoughtfully consider her answer.

"You see, Janell, it's important to debrief every round, match, and tournament. And I have found these 4 questions to be helpful in becoming your best:

1. What did I do well?
2. What did I learn?
3. What is my focus for this week in practice?
4. What will I do in the next match or tournament to demonstrate that I learned and grew from last week?

"I have shared these questions with many athletes to help them learn and grow from every performance or competition. And the first two questions drive the second two questions. When answering the first question, you must be specific and your list of answers should be longer than your answers to the second question. You should identify at least 3-5 things that you did well compared to one thing that you learned. You should strive for around a 5-1 ratio, or even higher if you can. Do you know why?"

"Because we tend to focus more on the negative things...things we didn't do well." Janell responded.

"That's right. And we discount the things that we did do well. We want to amplify and replicate the things we did well in our next performance, not downplay and discount them. And the second question has an interesting choice of words."

"I was thinking about that when you said it: 'What did you learn?'" Janell chimed in. "I don't think I have ever really considered what I learned from a tournament performance. I just thought about my score, whether I played good or bad, and what I did wrong."

Janell was learning to say the quiet part out loud. The thoughts, feelings, and emotions that she would often bury or not want to think about, process, and respond to.

In a world full of 30-second reels and hot-take moments, there is a tendency to *move on* than thoughtfully *move through* moments. It can be uncomfortable to stop and carefully consider what was learned in the process of both successful moments and setback moments – moments that could potentially set up you up for the next success if you truly learn from them.

"That's great insight, Janell! We often don't learn from moments and instead just focus on what we did wrong. Dwelling on our mistakes doesn't help us learn. I intentionally crafted this question to include the word 'learn.' The task is for you to think about a couple of things you could have done better and then summarize these areas of improvement into a single learning point. For example, you may have hit a couple of shots off target or into a hazard. Upon careful consideration, you realize that you did not go through your full pre-shot routine. The answer to 'What did you learn?' would be: 'When I consistently execute my pre-shot routine, I hit my best shots.' Do you see how powerful that can be? The goal is to learn from the moments when you don't do something as well as you can, not lament them."

"That makes a lot of sense, and I understand the power of these questions," Janell gratefully replied.

"These questions provide not only accountability and context for our coaching sessions but also guidance and structure for your own debriefs. I want you to take ownership of your debriefs and the learning that results from them. In all of the things I am teaching you, I want to show you how to leverage these principles to perform at your best...in golf and in life. And then I want you to share it with others. A great mentor once told me that true 'greatness is being the best you can be with a passionate purpose of making the lives of those around you better and inspiring them to do and be their best.'[2] You don't hoard greatness for yourself. You share greatness with others. And one of the ways you can do that is by always doing your best and inspiring others to do the same."

"That's what I want to do. Inspire and help others to be and do their best! I think that's what being a great leader is all about, and it's what God has called me to do," Janell replied enthusiastically.

"It's the highest ambition – to be a servant leader and thereby fulfill God's purpose for your life. Now, tell me about your round, but make sure to keep the questions in mind as you answer."

Janell took Mike through her last tournament being careful to answer the questions about what she did well and what she learned. She highlighted key moments in the round, certain holes and shots where she could have done better, and what she learned from this performance.

"That is a great debrief. What I heard you say is that you were consistent in your pre-shot routine, that you hit your driver well, and that you were specific in calling out your target and visualizing your shot."

"Yes," Janell replied. "And I improved my self-talk during this round by consistently using my activation phrase of 'Trust my shot!'"

"That's great," Mike said confirming that Janell was on the right path. "What did you learn?"

As she thought about the round, Janell said, "I think trust is the key. When I trust, I play my best my golf! When I wonder or fear if I can make a certain shot or if I overthink what I am trying to do, I play tentative and timid golf. And I am not a timid person or player!"

"Ok, well let's work on that. I think the theme of today's session will help you and will provide yet another key to building a championship mindset."

"I'm ready!" Janell said with anticipation about what the next key success factor would be.

"The third key to developing a championship mindset is:

Be Outcome-Driven and Process-Focused

KEY 3
Be Outcome-Driven
& Process-Focused

Key Word: *Process*

Mike took his notebook out and began to write 3 words across the top of the page – Worry, Focus, and Obsess. He then asked Janell, "Which word do you like best?"

"Focus," Janell answered decisively.

"Good. We are on the same page," Mike said confirming her guess. "He then drew a line and wrote 3 more words across the page under the initial words. The illustration looked something like this:

WORRY   FOCUS   OBSESS
____

CIRCUMSTANCES   PROCESS   OUTCOMES

He then put his hand over the middle two words and further explained, "The way our mind works, we can often jump back and forth either worrying about circumstances or obsessing about outcomes. And when I use the word 'Obsess,' I am talking about it in a negative sense. Like obsessing desperately over an outcome. Always remember there is fine line between determination and desperation. It's okay and even good to have a determined mindset and say things like, 'I will make this putt!' But what you don't want to do is to allow your fear to drive you to desperately control an outcome.

"The problem with a flippant mindset that jumps back and forth between worrying about circumstances and obsessing over outcomes is that we forget and forsake the middle part of this diagram, which is the key to being present in the moment. Focusing on the process to achieve the outcome that we want."

Mike finished by drawing a line connecting the dots from Focus to Process to Outcomes and wrote the following phrase underneath the words:

Outcome-Driven and Process-Focused

He paused to let Janell reflect on what he had drawn and then added. "I am not an artist, but I think you get the picture, the principle, and the point."

"Yes," Janell responded. "I understand it, and this makes sense. So how we do apply this to my golf game and, more specifically, my next tournament?"

"Well, I am glad you asked. That's a perfect transition to your next home-work assignment. I want you to write down some outcomes that you want to achieve. You could think of these as goals. They could be micro-goals like win the next tournament, shoot a certain score, or hit a certain shot. They could also be what I call macro-goals like win the District MVP, go to the State Tournament, or play college golf. For each goal, I want you to write down some process-oriented things that relate and are connected to achieving that goal. For example, if you want to shoot a score of 68 in a round, there are process-oriented things you need to focus on like being present and playing shot by shot, being consistent in your pre-shot routine, and visualizing your shot before you make it. Let's start with 3 outcomes or goals that you want to accomplish and 2-3 process-oriented things you need to focus on for each of those goals. How does that sound?"

"Sounds great, and I can do that!" Janell responded enthusiastically as she immediately began to think of goals she wanted to accomplish.

"And as far as your next tournament is concerned, I want you to be more process-focused than outcome-oriented or even outcome-ob-sessed," Mike said thinking that might get a reaction from Janell.

"Can you explain that? What does that mean? Are you telling me not to care about my score?" Janell asked with a puzzled look on her face.

"No, I didn't say don't care about your score. I said don't obsess over it. So often, we can get locked in on an outcome and that is all we think about. And then we desperately strive to make that outcome happen. We try to control it and everything around and related to it, leading to frustration when a situation or moment doesn't align with our vision.

"Think about your shots," Mike continued. "Does every shot you hit perfectly travel to your intended target?"

"No, it doesn't. That's what I thought you were going to help me accomplish. Perfection!" Janell jokingly said knowing perfection was not the goal.

"The only 'P' word we are talking about now is *process*. If you have a certain score that you want to shoot as a goal, that's great! Be determined to accomplish that. Just don't think about or obsess over it the entire round. Focus on the key factors – your success factors – to accomplish that goal. Be process-focused. Execute your pre-shot routine every time. Play shot to shot. Be present in the current moment. Don't focus on past holes or shots or ones in the future. Make the current moment that you are in count.

"And I have not found a pathway to perfection, and I doubt you ever will," Mike added. There was only one man who lived a perfect life!"

"Jesus," Janell said.

"That's right. Jesus!" Mike affirmed. "And by the way, while all of the things I am teaching and sharing with you can and will help on and off the course, Jesus is the one who can provide perfect peace in any moment. You need to rely on Him during your rounds."

"I struggle with that because I don't know if Jesus cares about sports. Do you think He cares about a golf score or my next tournament?" Janell asked, truly interested in solving this mystery.

"I believe He cares about you and everything that He has gifted you to do. I see too many people separate parts of their lives like sports and work because they think He only cares about and can help them with their spiritual life. We have been created with gifts and talents and have been given God-ordained moments to display those with excellence for God's glory. That includes everything. Every part of our life. And why would we not want to access His presence, power, and peace in a moment when we need it the most just because we are playing a game or sport?" Mike responded passionately and then added, "I love what Paul says in Colossians 3:17:

> *'And whatever you do, whether in word or deed, do it all in the name of the Lord Jesus, giving thanks to God the Father through him.'*

"This is a theme verse for me," Mike continued. "I love how Paul emphasizes 3 times the idea of everything. First, he uses the word 'everything,' which means **EVERYTHING**. He then further explains that he is talking about words and deeds, everything you say and everything you do. Finally, he uses the word 'all.' Do it all in the name of Jesus for the glory of God. This verse is a great litmus test for what we should be doing and how, and it rules out what we should not be doing."

"You're right, and I love that verse!" Janell responded.

Janell so appreciated how Mike incorporated faith into his approach for these coaching sessions. She was a person of faith and had accepted Jesus into her life. She knew she had been created by God on purpose for a purpose. When she was younger, she had decided that she wanted to live for Jesus and was so grateful that she had a relationship with Him. She wanted to know more about God and learn how to memorize Bible verses and apply them to her life.

"How do you know the Bible so well?" Janell asked.

"Outcome-Driven and Process-Focused!" Mike said with a smile bringing this part of the conversation back to today's lesson. "I want to know God in a deeper way and experience the presence of Jesus and His Holy Spirit in a more intimate way, so I pray that every day and then focus on the process of reading His Word and reflecting on what He is telling me. I journal, often writing these verses down to memorize and reflect."

"Sounds like a great process!" Janell said emphasizing the word 'process,' since Mike had made it clear that it was the word of the day. "I journal, and I read the Bible, but I need to do it more consistently."

"If you want to know God – not just know about Him – but truly know Him, investing time with Him through prayer and reading the Bible is the best way to begin your day! It's an eternal investment," Mike said as they wrapped up their coaching session. "You have your assignment. Go make the most of your moments!"

Janell left the coffee shop with much more than a homework assignment. She had just experienced a life lesson that would soon permeate every area of her life. Janell went home and pondered the depth of their discussion. She also reviewed and reflected on some additional questions that Mike had given her:

BE OUTCOME-DRIVEN & PROCESS-FOCUSED

- What are some outcomes you are pursuing in the macro moments of the season and the micro moments of individual games?

- What are process-oriented actions that will help you achieve those outcomes?

CHAPTER 6

Develop An "I Will" Mindset

After another couple of weeks passed, Mike and Janell met for another coaching session. This one was scheduled to be at her favorite golf course where she had invested so much time practicing her craft. Mike had told her in previous sessions that it was important to sit down and meet for the first few sessions to build the proper foundation. Coffee mixed with mental game coaching can be enlightening and provide just the right energy and insight to inspire your best.

Practice, competition, and tournaments provide the true test to see if these principles work. To discover if the right words, thoughts, and mindset can produce progress when it matters most.

Mike drove to the golf course, got out of his car, and walked toward the practice green where he saw Janell practicing her putts.

"Hey Mike! Watch this!" Janell said with confidence as she proceeded to drain a 25-foot putt.

"Wow! Impressive! With that much confidence and skill, what do you need me for?" Mike responded.

"It's because of you that I can make that putt. Our coaching sessions have taken my confidence and focus to another level that I didn't know I had."

"Well, I think you're being far too kind and giving me too much of the credit. All of this is inside of you. We are just finding the best way to unlock and unleash your talent and not let the enemy distract, discourage, or defeat you," Mike said.

"Let me finish a few more putts and then we can go out on the course," Janell responded, staying focused on the task at hand.

Janell had a skill of always making others feel better about themselves in her presence. She often deflected praise and redirected encouragement to the people around her. She looked for the greatness in others and then used words that would help them not only see it in themselves but also believe it to be true. She was humble and a servant leader, putting others before herself. And this posture truly endeared her to others. People loved being around Janell, because she made them feel better – about themselves, about the situation, and about whatever they were walking through that day.

As Janell was finishing her final practice putts, Mike asked her a question: "Janell, what are you thinking about when you stand over a putt?"

"Aren't you supposed to tell me what to think? I mean you are my mental coach!" Janell said with a slight bit of humor and sarcasm.

"Well, I think you should be thinking that you will make the putt. Every time!" Mike responded without hesitating. He then added, "I am asking YOU the question, because I want to know what is going on inside your mind. I need to know what you are thinking so we can make sure you are thinking the right thoughts. And I need you to be honest and authentic in that process and not just give me the answer you think I want to hear. Your honesty will allow us to collaborate effectively to help solve the puzzle of your peak performance and becoming your best."

"Puzzle, huh? Is what I shoot and how I play a puzzle?" Janell asked inquisitively. She had never heard that word or phrase before and wondered what Mike was trying to communicate when he talked about the "puzzle of peak performance."

"Yes, it is," Mike said definitively. "You have to look at your performance – past, present, and future – as a puzzle because puzzles can be solved. When you look at trying to win a tournament or shoot a certain score or hit a given shot with a *fixed* mindset, you look at it with a win-lose mindset. Either you do it or don't do it, and sometimes this can lead to thinking that you can't do it at all. If you're not careful, this kind of thinking spirals into an absolute statement like 'I can't hit my driver,' or 'I can't perform in big moments.'

"When you look at performance and becoming your best as a puzzle to be solved, you look at the current situation through the lens of a *growth* mindset filled with curiosity about how to solve the situation in front of you," Mike continued. "In fact, you begin to say things to yourself like 'I can hit this shot, and here's how,' or 'I can win this tournament, and this is what I am going to do to achieve it.' And eventually, over time, your 'I can' turns into an 'I Will!' which is the next key to a championship mindset that we will talk about today."

"I never thought about it that way. And you're right, puzzles always have a solution. You just have to look for ways to solve them," Janell replied.

"And one more thing. Janell, it's a process."

"Wow! You just had to say that once again! 'It's a process.' For once, I would love for us to work on something that just instantly results in an immediate outcome! The process of waiting is hard."

"Yes, it is. But I love what Jon Gordon says about the process. He basically states that if you can learn to enjoy and love the process, you will love what the process produces in terms of the desired outcomes, success, and goals you want to achieve. Let's get started with today's session."

"Oh, I thought we already had," Janell said with a smile and an acknowledgement of the teachable moment that had just occurred.

Janell and Mike got in the golf cart and headed to the first tee.

"Hi Janell. Are you the 1:10 group?" the starter asked acknowledging the start time for the next group to tee off.

"Hi Coach," Janell said. "Yes, we are. This is Mike. He's my mental performance coach for golf."

Mike was startled for a second. He heard Janell refer to him as her mental performance coach. What a revelation and acknowledgment, and an indication of just how far she had come in realizing that there is purpose and power in not only identifying and revealing your fears but also having someone to help you face them. This discovery by Janell was quite different from a few months ago when she didn't even want to meet with him or any other mental performance coach.

After his reflection, Mike said, "It's great to meet you!"

"Mental Performance Coach. For Golf. Well, golf is a mental game! I didn't know they had coaches for that. Back when I was coaching, you just had to suffer with your shots and thoughts and hope to make it through the round," said the Starter.

Janell explained, "Coach was a golf coach for many years at a high school in West Texas. He moved to Katy, Texas, when his son got married, and he's been here ever since as the Starter for this course. He also serves as my full-time encourager who sometimes gives me golf tips...if I'm lucky."

"Oh, you don't need any tips from me, Janell!" Coach said, deflecting the praise. And then turning to Mike, he said, "She's got one of the most beautiful swings I have ever seen...and I have seen some good ones!"

"Oh, Coach! You're just saying that. I bet you say that to all the golfers that hit off this first tee," Janell chimed in.

"No, I don't. If it's one thing I am, I am honest and I don't pass out compliments to anyone. And believe me, in all of the years I have been working here, I have seen some really bad swings off this first tee."

All three laughed, then Janell and Mike drove up to the tee box. Coach shouted one last word to her, "Janell, make it count!"

Coach had always said that to Janell before every practice round. "Make it Count!" What an awesome and powerful phrase composed of just three words.

"Make" – a recognition that we have agency in life to do things and create moments that matter. In golf and in any area of life.

The second word of "it" seems generic, but it is an all-encompassing word for not only the round you are getting ready to step into but also for your life and all of the roles you play. The goals you have in front of you and the tasks you are invited to accomplish.

And whatever "IT" is, make it "COUNT!" Bring your best to that moment. Lay it all on the line. Be ALL IN! Be fully engaged, and be sure that your contribution, your performance, and ultimately your life counts for what matters most when all is said and done.

Janell got out of the cart and walked up to the first tee box. She looked around and surveyed the moment. She was soaking up the sun that was shining down on them, the trees that flowed with a slight wind, the beauty of being on a course, and the joy of being able to play a game she loved. She then turned toward the fairway of the first hole.

"So, tell me about this hole. What do you see, and what's your strategy?" Mike asked. He had played this hole and this course several times before but wanted to get inside of Janell's thought process – what did she see and what was she planning to do.

"Well, as you know, this hole is a dogwood left to the hole, so I like to hit a slight fade from right to left to position myself just beyond the trees and in striking distance for my approach shot," Janell responded with a well-conceived plan.

"That's sounds great. Let's see it!" Mike said encouragingly.

Janell went her through her pre-shot routine, took a practice swing, and then hit a shot in the fairway but that was about 10-15 yards short of her target distance. It was a nice shot but was not exactly what she wanted.

"Well, that's a little short of where I wanted to go," Janell said as she walked back to the cart.

"That's okay. You're still in the fairway, and I love your swing! Coach, the Starter, was right. You have one of the most natural and beautiful golf swings I have ever seen! How did you feel about that shot?" Mike asked wanting to get insight into what Janell might be thinking after a shot that was good but not perfect. This line of questioning would lay the groundwork for future sessions and future moments about training your mind to be present without lamenting the past or fearing the future.

"It was good, but not my best," Janell answered.

"I asked you a different question. I didn't ask you to critique the shot. I asked how you felt about the shot."

When it comes to mental performance, many people can buy into the lie that feelings are bad and should be stuffed down deep inside never to be heard from again. But feelings provide information and can lead you to the right place if you know how to process your feelings. You are not a robot. You have feelings, which provide insight about who you are and what you are experiencing in a given moment.

In his book *Do Hard Things*, performance expert Steve Magness says, "Feelings send a message, conveying information and nudging us toward a behavior."[2] He goes on to say that "Feelings are subject to distortion. They depend on context and interpretation. The better we're able to interpret, the better our ultimate decision."

We must develop the ability to identify, discern, and process our feelings in order to choose the best response.

Janell reflected on the distinction Mike was making about her feelings and then asked, "Why do I need to talk about my feelings? I thought we were focusing on my mind, not my heart. My thoughts, not my emotions."

"Because feelings can affect our behavior. We have to identify what we are feeling in order to process that emotion and choose a better response. We will talk about responding in our next coaching session, but before we can move on to that, I need you to be emotionally aware," Mike explained.

This on-course coaching session would transform Janell's view of emotions and feelings. She learned that emotions and feelings could be useful rather than distracting. She began to recognize, identify, and learn from them. Janell also realized that she was not a victim to her feelings nor did she have to be anchored to them. Instead, she understood that she had a choice and could identify her feelings and process them effectively. She discovered that her feelings don't define her, and they definitely should not determine her performance. She was excited about learning how to respond to them in the next coaching session with Mike.

"Ok, I felt frustrated that I did not hit the shot that I had pictured in my mind," Janell revealed.

"That you weren't perfect!" Mike said trying to tie further meaning to what she was revealing.

"I guess you could say that."

"Janell, the great sports psychologist Dr. Bob Rotella said that 'Golf is not a game of perfect.'"[3]

"I know! He wrote a whole book about it, and I read it," Janell replied.

"That's great! So, you know that golf, as well as life, is about managing imperfect moments rather than achieving flawless shots and perfect days," Mike further clarified.

"True! But it is hard. I put so much into my practices, and I want to show what I can do when it matters most," Janell shared.

"You can still do that and be able to deal with the imperfection. The truth is...we are not perfect, and we will never experience perfect days. It should not prevent you from having an 'I Will' Mindset."

"What's that?" Janell asked.

"It's the fourth key to a championship mindset," Mike said with a smile almost like he was waiting for right moment to get in the next teachable moment of the day.

The fourth key to a championship mindset is:

Develop an "I Will" Mindset

KEY 4
Develop an "I Will" Mindset

Key Word: *Determination*

"Okay, it's the fourth key. What is it? How do you develop an "I Will" Mindset?" Janell asked wanting to know more.

"I will tell you after you make this next shot," Mike responded.

"Holding out on me!" Janell said.

"No, just waiting for the right moment! Walk me through this approach shot," Mike said, redirecting the focus of this conversation back to golf.

"Ok, because I didn't hit my tee shot where I wanted it…"

"Wait," Mike interrupted. "I did not ask you about your tee shot. I asked you about this shot. Remember, we are working on being present in the moment. Nothing about that shot can help you with this shot, including how you felt about it. The only thing that matters is this moment. Tell me what you see on this shot and what you will do with it."

"You're right!" Janell confirmed. "I see trees slightly ahead on the left and sand on the other side of the fairway leading up to the green. I plan to hit a slight right to left shot that gets me to the green."

"I will," Mike said.

Confused by his response, Janell asked, "Wait, what? You will?"

"No, I said 'I will!'" Mike clarified. "You said, 'I plan,' and I suggest you change that to 'I Will!' I Will hit a slight right to left shot. And I would further suggest that you be more specific on your ultimate target. In other words, the goal is not to get on or to the green. The goal is to hit a shot that lands a few feet from the hole. Or in the hole if you are dreaming big. The more specific and determined you are about your goal and ultimate destination, the more likely you are to accomplish your goal and arrive at your intended destination. This is true in golf and in life."

"As are most things that you say!" Janell said with a smile. "Ok, I will hit a shot that draws right to left and rolls onto the green about 5-7 feet from the hole. Is that specific enough for you?"

"You are not saying it for me. You are declaring it for you. Now, go through your pre-shot routine, take a deep breath, and make it count. Remember, all that matters is this moment."

Janell stood back and pictured the shot she wanted to hit, went through her pre-shot routine, and took a deep breath before walking up to her golf ball and shooting a beautiful draw that started right and then gently curved around the trees up to the green about 10 feet from the hole.

Janell and Mike got back in the cart and drove up to the green to find the ball within reach of a sinkable putt.

Mike asked the obvious question, "How did you feel about that shot?"

"A lot better!" Janell responded.

"What do you think made the difference between your tee shot and that approach shot?" Mike asked wanting to lead her to discover the right answers for herself.

"My mindset and my commitment to the shot. I thought about what I wanted to do with it, pictured a more specific shot in my mind in terms of my target and the shape and trajectory of the shot, and then committed fully to making the shot I had just pictured in my mind," Janell explained.

"That's right," Mike affirmed. "When you are specific about your picture and committed to painting that picture like an artist, you shift to a mindset of trust and put yourself in the best position to be successful. The goal for a round is to then do that shot by shot and moment by moment."

"I understand," Janell confirmed. "There have probably been times in a round or tournament where I have not visualized my shot as specifically as I could or fully committed to certain shots. Sometimes, negative thoughts got in the way. Sometimes, I was distracted by other people on the course or was too worried about the score or past moments and so I was not fully present in the current moment."

"That's great insight. Now finish the job!" Mike encouraged.

Janell walked up to the putt, went through her routine, and knocked in the putt for a birdie.

In sports and in life, it is tempting to judge how things are going by a single moment in time. Feelings and sentiments can be affected and ruled by that moment. When the moment is good, you feel good about how things are going, but when it is not good, you feel bad and tend to allow that moment to put a cloud over everything you are attempting to do. A clouded mind discredits success in the past and casts doubt about your ability to have success in future moments. You will never know how things can turn out if you don't focus on being present in the moment with the right choices about your thoughts, your attitude, and your response.

Janell could have judged how she was doing by a tee shot that was not perfect. And this would have affected the next shot and the next shot becoming a self-fulfilling prophecy of a bad hole leading to an even worse round of golf. Instead, Janell learned that one shot doesn't define her – just like one moment doesn't define her – in terms of what she is capable of doing with the next shot, the next day, or the rest of her life.

"I love birdies!" Janell said as she reached into the cup and picked up her ball.

"Are you ready for me to tell you more about the fourth key to a championship mindset – developing an 'I Will' mindset?" Mike asked, eager to reveal the next principle and sensing this was the right moment.

"Yes, I have been waiting," Janell responded.

"You just demonstrated an 'I Will' mindset on those last 2 shots. In sports psychology, there is a continuum called the Volition Scale. Volition is just a big word for your will or desire to do something."

Mike then took out his notebook and drew something like this:

VOLITION
The will or desire to do something; determination

"The Volition Scale measures your ability to maintain focus, persevere through challenges, and achieve your goals despite internal or external obstacles," Mike said pointing to what he just drew. "In golf and in life, the path will be filled with challenges that attempt to detour you from accomplishing your goals. Fear, doubt, and anxiety will try to creep in and tell you that you are not good enough. External factors like the weather and obstacles on the course will attempt to distract you from your target. In any of these scenarios, you will be faced with a choice concerning your will or desire to accomplish the goal. Possible responses include:

- I Won't.
- I Can't.
- I'd Like To.
- I'll Try.
- I Can.
- I Will.

"And I think you would agree with me that 'I Won't' is the worst and 'I Will' is the best response. Yet, this middle option of 'I'll Try' can a be destructive choice that leads to a downward spiral filled with little to no commitment. 'I'll Try' can lead to a vicious cycle of spinning and constantly 'trying,' whatever that means. As Yoda said in Star Wars, 'Do, or Do Not. There is no try!'"

"So 'I Will' is the right response," Janell said as she reflected on the graphic.

"Yes," Mike confirmed. "For every shot that you take in a tournament round or even in practice, you need to evaluate where you are on this continuum and strive for an 'I Will' mindset, beginning with your self-talk," Mike added.

"Can you say more about that? How an 'I Will' mindset begins with your self-talk?" Janell asked inquisitively.

"Somewhere in your pre-shot routine before you act like an artist and paint the picture you just envisioned in your mind, you need to say to yourself, 'I Will make this shot.' This could be literally or figuratively through your activation phrase. For example, you could say the words 'I Will' or you could say something like 'Trust my shot' which infers full commitment and trust to accomplish the task. Self-talk, body language, attitude, and facial expressions are all external reflections of an inward condition and posture that indicate where you are on the volition scale and if you are fully committed...or not."

"So what I hear you saying is that in one way or another, I should be saying 'I Will' make every shot. That seems like perfection, and we just talked about how every shot won't be perfect and how I should not expect perfection," Janell said, working through in her mind how to apply this new principle.

"It's not about perfection. It's about perspective, commitment, and learning to live with the results," Mike clarified.

"Ok, help me understand that," Janell said.

"Let me share a story with you that might help. When I was working with a professional baseball team, some of the players came up to me and said, 'We deal with failure every day.' I asked them to tell me more about that. They went on to explain that a good batting average in the major leagues is around .300. That means that they are only 'succeeding' 3 out of 10 times and 'failing' – not succeeding or getting a hit – 7 out of 10 times. I told them about the Volition Scale and the power of having an 'I Will' mindset. We aligned on the fact that you can't step into the batter's box attempting to hit a 100-mph fastball with an 'I'll

Try' mindset. You can't back off from the goal of 'I Will' just because it did not happen in a previous at bat or moment.

"When you nurture the right perspective and understand the law of averages in your sport, you gain a true and proper view of the importance of moments. You understand that you are not defined by your performance and that your worth does not depend on a golf shot.

"From a more granular point of view, you can nurture a perspective that knows every shot will not be perfect. You begin to understand that even the best golfers, and really athletes in any sport, don't make 100% of their shots. For example, take Steph Curry, who is one of the best shooters in the world. It's easy to falsely believe that he hits every shot that he attempts. In reality, his career shooting percentage is 47%, which is great, but it is not 100%. For a golfer like Scottie Scheffler, his driving accuracy is around 62-64% off the tee. So why should you think that you are going to make 100% of the shots you take if the best in sports cannot do it?

"A proper perspective prepares the way for you to not be shocked when a shot doesn't go as planned but rather be able to move on to the next shot or hole," Mike continued. "While you may not be happy about bad and unexpected moments, the right perspective allows you to put the past behind you and be present in the current moment. It allows you to say 'I Will,' even when you just had a moment where you *did not*!"

"So I am not lying to myself when I say, 'I Will.' I am just committing to the moment that is right in front of me," Janell said with conviction.

"That's right!" Mike agreed. "See, you are already developing a deep understanding of these keys and once they become a part of who you are, you will begin to see the fruit of a championship mindset, which doesn't mean always winning the trophy, award, or ring. A championship mindset fuels a life of significance freeing you to live the victorious life that God created you for...on purpose for a purpose because of Jesus, the ultimate champion on the cross. I love what Paul talks about in Philippians 4:6-8:

> *⁶Do not be anxious about anything, but in every situation, by prayer and petition, with thanksgiving, present your requests to God. ⁷And the peace of God, which transcends all understanding, will guard your hearts and your minds in Christ Jesus.*
> *⁸Finally, brothers and sisters, whatever is true, whatever is noble, whatever is right, whatever is pure, whatever is lovely, whatever is admirable—if anything is excellent or praiseworthy—think about such things.'*

"Paul provides the blueprint for the *things* you need to be thinking about on the golf course. Thoughts that are positive, productive, and lead to peace and your best performance. You need to guard your heart against any person, thought, circumstance, or situation that tries to distract and divert your attention from the moment right in front of you.

"I also love this quote from speaker, author, and friend Rebekah Lyons about perspective. She says,

> *'In the quiet we gain perspective. Our thoughts shape our perspective, and our perspective shapes our attitude.'⁴*

"Your perspective – the right perspective – is not developed in reaction to or in the midst of moments where you are required to perform," Mike explained. "It is nurtured and cultivated in the quiet moments of preparation well before you walk up to the first tee. The moments that no one sees except you and God. The moments when you reflect on who you are and who you are becoming. The space where you invest time to grow mentally, physically, emotionally and most of all, spiritually.

"It's in the quiet moments that purpose and greatness call to you in a whisper to show you what you are capable of, or better said, what God is capable of doing in and through you," Mike continued. "Don't neglect those moments. Leverage them. Invest in them, and you will play and live from an 'I Will' posture in everything that you do."

"I Will!" Janell said with a smile.

Mike laughed and said, "You are a great student! Now, let's play a few more holes, and let me see your 'I Will' spirit on these next shots."

Janell and Mike got back in the cart and played a few more holes. Mike was amazed at what he observed. Janell had such a great combination of skills including an ability to envision her shot, choose the right club, and hit her shot with precision and accuracy. She also had a determined spirit and a quiet toughness. She showed joy in everything she did, including playing a game that can be very challenging mentally.

She had an organic, natural, and effortless swing built by the many hours of practice. She was content but not satisfied, so she continued to work on her craft to see how good she could become. Her preparation was unleashing her potential.

Peak performers in sports, business, and life understand what it takes to become their best. It is a balance of grit and grace. A combination of contentment and commitment. If you overemphasize the grit piece, you will always be grinding toward a goal that seems out of reach and never be content with who you are and what you have accomplished. Grace is needed in the moments where you don't excel to develop a proper perspective, nurture your mental health, and allow you to be present in the next moment to perform at your best.

Mike and Janell finished up the day and headed to the clubhouse.

"This was a great day...or 'moment' as you like to say," Janell said, reflecting on all that she had learned.

"Yes, today was a great moment!" Mike confirmed.

"You said there were 5 keys to a championship mindset that you were going to share with me. When do I get to learn about the fifth key?" Janell asked.

"You will have to wait until the next session," Mike answered.

"Leaving me in suspense, huh?" Janell replied.

"Yes, I am. Have a great rest of your day!"

Mike headed to his car, but Janell stayed in the clubhouse, opened her journal, and wrote down a few things that Mike had said were critical to developing an "I Will" mindset:

KEYS TO DEVELOPING AN "I WILL" MINDSET

- Nurturing Perspective

- Be Present in the Moment

- Be Willing to Live with the Results

- Be Fully Engaged in the Process

- Choose Positive & Productive Thoughts

She also journaled answers to the following questions:

DEVELOP AN "I WILL" MINDSET

- How can you develop more of an "I Will" Mindset in any moment?

- How does having a proper perspective and being willing to live with the result help you develop a determined mindset?

Finally, she developed her "I Will" statements:

- I Will trust my shots.

- I Will have a great attitude in everything I do.

- I Will practice with a purpose.

- I Will be a servant leader encouraging those that God puts in my path.

- I Will glorify God by giving my best in all things.

- I Will hold on to my plans loosely and pursue God's plans fiercely.

- I Will honor my parents and enjoy the moments with my family.

- I Will be present in the moment.

Every day, Janell pursued personal growth. On the course and off. In practice and in tournaments. In the classroom and at home. This year would reveal even more about who Janell was becoming and what she was capable of doing...all because of the work she was investing in the moments no one could see.

More Questions

The girls interrupted Janell's story, "Coach JJ! Coach JJ! We have a few more questions!"

"Ok, what are your questions?" Janell patiently replied.

"You talked a lot about perfection and another word, perspective, with Coach Mike," Reagan said. "Can you tell us more about these words and what they mean?"

"Yes, Coach JJ," Meredith chimed in. "I want to make every shot I hit a great one. And sometimes when I don't, I get frustrated, and then I start to doubt myself."

"Yes, I can relate because I want all my shots to be perfect. I had to learn to develop a proper perspective in golf and in life. You see girls, we all want to do our best. And when we compete, we want to be the best. When something or someone gets in the way of that, we can get frustrated or think we are not good enough. We begin to focus on what others have or what others do rather than being grateful for who we are and the things we have been given.

"And perfection is just a misaligned expectation," Janell continued.

"What does misaligned mean?" Meredith asked.

"Misaligned means that your expectation of perfection does not line up with the truth that we are not perfect. Some shots will go into the trees. Some shots will go into the sand or water. When those moments happen, you can't get frustrated."

"How do we not get frustrated when a bad shot happens?" Reagan asked.

"Yes, especially if we said, 'I Will!' like Coach Mike told you to say?" Meredith asked, showing that she had been listening to Janell's story.

"The power of a proper perspective helps us manage our expectations to realize that not all of the shots we hit will go where we want them to go," Janell explained. "When I learned to temper my expectations of perfection and choose a proper perspective, I was able to play loose, fierce, and free. I was able to hit every shot with trust and full commitment because I was willing to live with the results.

"My faith also provided a solid foundation for me because I knew that God had given me talent and opportunities to glorify Him. I felt His presence in the heat of competition, and I knew He was with me giving me peace in the process. I learned from Coach Mike that if faith forms the essence of who I am, I need to rely on my faith in everything I do and that who I am spiritually must permeate every area of my life... including golf. I even put my favorite Bible verse in prominent places including as a patch on my high school varsity letter jacket to remind me of who was guiding and directing the steps in my journey on and off the course.

"Overall, I learned that a proper perspective prevents you from judging your worth by one shot or by one moment and encourages you to trust that you can and will hit shots that go exactly where you want them to go."

"So, what you are saying is that we need to have an 'I Will' mindset before each shot and not get upset if the shot is not perfect?" Reagan confirmed.

"Yes, Reagan," Janell confirmed. "The power of pre-deciding what you will think and how you will respond when a negative moment happens is so powerful. When unexpected and negative moments occur during a tournament, you are prepared to respond in the right way."

"Can you tell us more about how to do that?" Meredith asked.

"Yes, I can," Janell responded. "Let me continue with the story, and I think it will become clearer how to do this. How I *learned* to do this."

CHAPTER 7

Janell's Junior Year

*"Learn from the past. Prepare for the future.
Perform in the moment."*

MIKE VAN HOOZER, <u>MOMENTS: MAKING YOUR LIFE
COUNT FOR WHAT MATTERS MOST</u>

Several months went by after the initial meeting with Mike. Janell started her junior year – a year filled with possibilities and potential. In your junior year, you are not a freshman still trying to figure things out. You have progressed through your sophomore year, which can sometimes be a time of discovery or a moment of going through the motions. By your junior year, you have discovered more about yourself, your identity, and your potential. You are in a prime spot to put your mark on the rest of your high school career.

Janell was filled with excitement, curiosity, and a renewed sense of purpose. As she attended her classes and caught up with friends about what they had done this past summer, she also pondered her path. She reminisced about family time and vacations. By now, she had experienced a few more coaching sessions with Mike to work on her mental game. She also had played in some tournaments and applied some of the keys she had learned from him including playing from a posture of belief and trust, not tying her identity to her performance, and focusing on what she could control.

After their first meeting, Janell expected to have immediate success. When she did not experience transformational results immediately based on her new mindset, she shared her frustration with Mike in their next mental game session. Mike reminded her, "Janell, growth is a process."

We often want immediate success. We want to read books about *Five Steps to the Summit* or more appropriately named, *Five Easy Steps to the Summit*. We consume content searching for hacks that are quick to implement but often leaving us wanting more because they do not produce longer-term value and impact. Growth is found in spaced and purposeful repetition. When we apply insights to action over time in a meaningful way, we see growth in our abilities and in our ability to achieve and to become the person God created us to be.

As the school day ended, Janell anticipated the opportunities of the upcoming year. She sensed that she was changing, growing, and becoming a better person, golfer, and leader.

She grabbed something to eat on the way to the course and began to practice. She focused on putting first, then chipping, and then went onto the range for some longer shots with the rest of her clubs. She finished her practice session playing 9 holes of golf.

As she got ready to leave, the golf pro was driving up in a cart. "Hi Janell! How was your practice?"

"It was a good day! How are you doing?" Janell responded.

"I am doing great. It's your junior year. Are you excited?"

"Yes! Yes, I am!" Janell said. "I want to build on what I have done in the past and keep growing and getting better. I am looking forward to the opportunity of another year of playing the game I love!"

Janell realized that she was starting to use some of the language that she was working on with Mike in their mental game sessions. Growth. Building on lessons learned from the past. Viewing challenges as opportunities. The keys were beginning to stick in her mind, formulating a new vocabulary and new mental pathways to help her pursue her best in golf and in life.

Layne responded, "Well, we are all cheering for you and are here for you. You are a great golfer and an even better person. Enjoy this time!"

Layne had recognized Janell's talent and potential when she was younger and had even invested in teaching her the game through individual golf lessons.

"Thanks Layne! I appreciate it. See you tomorrow," Janell responded.

Janell had appreciated the lessons Layne had taught her and was encouraged to have people in her corner that were cheering her on. She knew life was not about her but about the higher purpose of glorifying God with her talents and making a positive impact in the lives of others.

Janell left the course and headed to Starbucks to meet Mike for another mental game coaching session. In preparation for this session, she had been reading through a workbook that he had given her to help complement their in-person sessions. So far, they had covered the following concepts:

- Your identity is not tied to your performance.
- Being present shot to shot is the goal.
- Be outcome-driven and process-focused.

- Focus on what you can control, influence what you can, and flush the rest.

Today's session involved going over some "homework" that was assigned in their last coaching session.

"How was your day?" Mike asked as Janell entered the coffee shop and sat down at the table.

"It was great. I got in some good practice today. I also got to invest in my best buddy. How was your day?" Janell asked.

"I had a great day," Mike responded. "What is a Best Buddy?"

"Oh, it's a program that pairs student volunteers with students who have challenges intellectually and developmentally. I have been a volunteer and have been paired with my buddy since 4th grade," Janell responded.

"That's so cool! It's awesome that you make time to invest in the life of another person like this. Did you do your homework?"

"I did," Janell responded.

After their last coaching session of the summer, Mike had given Janell a homework assignment. He asked her to develop what he called an "activating phrase," a phrase that would activate something physical or technical for her. This phrase would help her connect the mental work that they were doing with the technical work she was doing by herself and with her coaches. He explained that this phrase would be the key to helping her be fearless and focused in any moment.

In sports and in life, we need meaningful phrases that go beyond a cliché or a mantra. Words are powerful, especially when they have depth and meaning, and therefore impact because we know what they represent.

For an athlete in the heat of competition, simplification is important to avoid overthinking. Just like athletes, everyone can experience overthinking, which occurs when the mind begins to consider all the steps that lead to an outcome. Overthinking can also lead to striving to force or control the outcome or result. Instead of overthinking about all of the steps to success, an activating phrase can help you simplify a plethora of thoughts into a 2-3 word phrase that summarizes the details and allows you to stay focused on what matters most...in sports and in life.

"Well, what did you choose for your activating phrase?" Mike asked with curiosity.

Janell looked at the notes on her phone and answered, "I chose 2 phrases. My go-to phrase is 'Trust My Shot!' and the second one is: 'Be Athletic.'"

Mike thought about the 2 phrases she had chosen and said, "Those are great phrases. Tell me more about why you selected them and how you intend to use them."

"I chose 'Trust My Shot!' as my go-to activating phrase because it encompasses all that we have been working on in these mental game sessions and all that I need to do when I am on the course. I don't need to be over-thinking on the course! I need to trust my shot... moment by moment."

Janell smiled as she said the last part of this phrase as she knew Mike liked to use the word *moments* and had repeatedly preached the power of this word in sports and in life.

"Trust my shot is a great phrase, and I love that you incorporated the mantra of playing shot to shot and being present in the moment."

Mike realized that these principles were becoming alive in Janell's life and that she was beginning to master the power of being present and unleashing her gifts and talents to make a positive difference in the world. He noticed that Janell was relentlessly focusing on excellence in everything she said and did to inspire others to do the same and to shine a spotlight on God, who created her and blessed her with these talents. Janell's faith was the foundation of her life and helped her discern that she was created on purpose for a purpose.

"Janell, tell me about your second activating phrase," Mike said, returning to the current moment.

"I chose 'Be Athletic' as a secondary phrase to use when technical thoughts try to overcrowd my mind and hinder me from truly being an artist on the golf course. I feel that this phrase will allow me to unleash my technique in the moment and to play loose, fierce, and free."

"I love it! You did an excellent job on your homework. Are you ready to learn about the fifth key to a championship mindset?"

"Yes, I have been wondering when you were going to do the big reveal!" Janell said with a smile and a scoop of sarcasm.

"It's time! And it is something we have talked about in some of our previous coaching sessions. The fifth key to a championship mindset is:

Improve Recovery Time

KEY 5

Improve Recovery Time

Key Word: *Resiliency*

"This may be one of the most practical and relevant of the five keys I have shared with you. 'Recovery time' can be a huge X-Factor for you in the heat of competition. Your ability to 'recover' from an unexpected moment and be present in the current moment with a positive and productive mindset truly allows you to play shot to shot. Have there been times on the course and in your life when you have experienced a frustrating or disappointing moment?"

"Yes! I think everyone experiences those types of moments in golf and in life," Janell said without hesitation. "We don't live in a perfect world, so we are going to feel the effects of imperfection at some point in our lives...sometimes multiple unexpected moments in a round of golf or in a typical day."

"And have you ever let those moments linger longer than they should? Have you ever let the fear and frustration of a valley moment affect your focus and faithfulness in a current or future moment, preventing you from playing at your best?" Mike said, continuing to probe.

"Yes. If I am being honest, I have let bad moments affect what I am doing in the current moment," Janell answered.

"I believe everyone can be enticed and tricked into doing that. Why do you think that is?" Mike asked.

"For me, I can sometimes lament the past, regretting what I could have done and maybe should have done. I get discouraged and wonder why a bad shot or a bad moment occurred. And from a spiritual perspective, I can be tempted to blame God for what happened or wonder how He could have allowed it to happen. It's like I shake my fist at the sky both figuratively and sometimes literally," Janell revealed.

"That's so true, Janell. And is that helpful?"

"It's helpful to get it out and not suppress my feelings and emotions, but it is not helpful to 'linger' there, as you said, for too long," Janell responded.

"That's right," Mike affirmed. "Lingering in lament over past moments and shots that you can do nothing about now is not helpful or productive. It keeps you from being present in the current moment – the moment that you have the ability and agency to affect and influence. That's why recovery time is so important.

"I define 'recovery time' as the time it takes you to move from a moment that you did not expect to happen into the current moment. It's a qualitative measure, not quantitative, meaning that I am not going to get out there and measure it with a stopwatch or timer on my phone. I am not going to say, 'Ok, Janell, it's been five minutes, and you are still thinking about the last shot that went in the trees.' Rather, it is something that is qualitative in nature. Recovery time is something that you feel and sense and a tempo that you know and can refine. You will never perfect it, but you will be able to become better at managing it over time as you learn the tools and techniques that we are working on to improve your recovery time. And Janell..." Mike paused for effect and her response.

"Yes?" Janell responded with a curious face.

"It's a process!" Mike said.

"I should have known you were going to say that!" Janell responded emphatically. "Teach me how to improve my recovery time."

"There are two R phrases that will help you improve your recovery time. The first phrase is:

Respond, not react

"When a bad or unexpected moment happens, our first tendency is to react. And most of the time, we react emotionally, which is not productive. Reacting emotionally leads to a spiraling downward in performance. It looks like this."

Mike took a page out of his notebook and began to draw something like this:

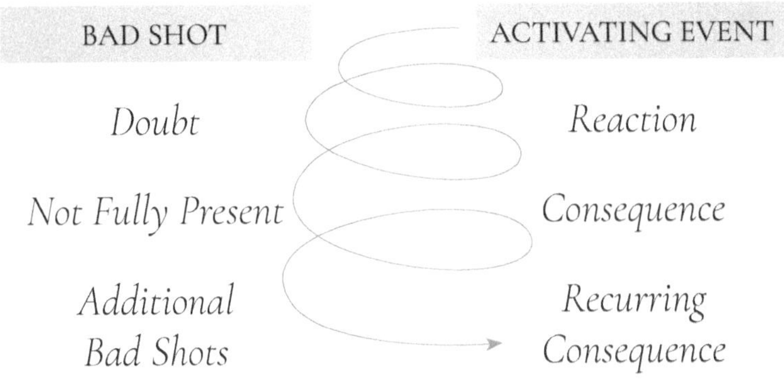

"The activating event is something that happens during a round like a bad shot into the trees," Mike explained. "If you are not careful, your first tendency can be to react emotionally to that event which allows negative thoughts and doubt to creep in. You are worrying about the shot that just unfortunately happened, resulting in a consequence of not being fully present for your next shot. And this can lead to additional bad shots. Your performance spirals downward creating a bad cycle, which may occur for a few more shots, a few more holes, or the rest of your round."

Janell jumped in and said, "I have definitely experienced that downward spiral. My question for you is: How do I break the cycle? Especially in the middle of a round?"

"Well, the good news is that you have a choice about what you think. And as we have discussed before, what you choose to focus on magnifies in size," Mike answered.

"Yes, I remember that and have been applying that in some of my previous tournaments, especially when it comes to visualizing my shot."

"That's great! Choosing the right thought before you hit your shot is a proactive way to use it to your advantage. As it relates to improving your recovery time, you can use it as a response versus a reaction. You can choose a better response," Mike said.

In his book The Seven Habits of Highly Effective People, Stephen Covey wrote, "Between stimulus and response is our greatest power – the freedom to choose." He furthers defines the word responsibility as "response-ability, or the ability to choose your response."

Covey explains, "Highly proactive people recognize that responsibility. They do not blame circumstances, conditions, or conditioning for their behavior. Their behavior is a product of their own conscious choice, based on values, rather than a product of their conditions, based on feeling."[2]

You have agency in your life to choose the best response in every moment in your life. While your initial impulse may be to react or to lash out, you have been created with self-awareness, imagination, conscience, and an independent will to choose the right response.

Mike continued to add to the drawing, inserting this section above what he had just drawn:

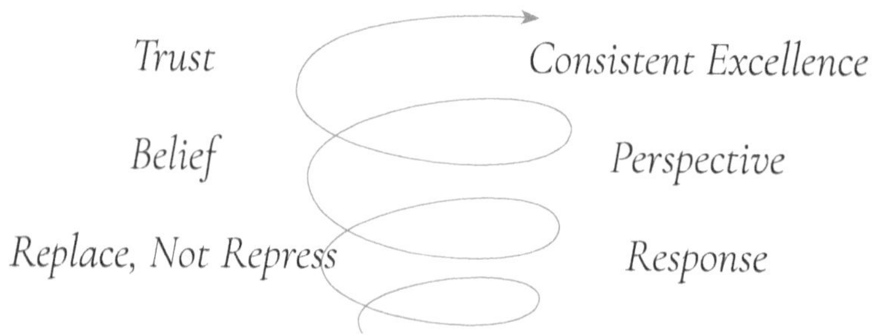

"Instead of reacting emotionally to an unexpected event, you can choose to respond, not react. And it involves the second R phrase:

Replace, not Repress

"In our first meeting, I asked if you had ever been in a pool and we talked about the five forces of fear, pressure, doubt, negative thoughts, and lack of confidence. I talked about a beach ball as a visual metaphor for these five forces. I explained when you try to repress negative forces and thoughts, they resurface in our mind similar to the beach ball that resurfaces when we try to press it below the water. Instead of repressing our thoughts and feelings, we can process them and then replace the negative thought or sense of fear and doubt with what we call an 'activating phrase.'"

"My homework assignment!" Janell jumped in.

"Yes, that was your homework assignment, and you did a great job with it even though I had not given you the full explanation of the principle. I had not given you the 'full reveal,' as you said earlier," Mike said with a smile.

Mike continued, "A great activating phrase is a 2-3 word phrase that activates something physical or technical for you related to the outcome you are working to achieve. The phrases you chose are great because they fit this description.

"A great activating phrase contains depth. What I mean is the phrase should not be fluffy and should provide a foundation to achieve success. While a phrase like 'You're Special' is nice and something you want your friends and family to say about you, it is not specific enough to activate your mind and direct your actions in the moment when you are hitting your shot. An activating phrase with depth is specific enough to trigger the right physical response, broad enough to encapsulate and simplify the technique you have been working on, and effective enough to help you unleash your talent with freedom and trust.

"On game day, it's important to simplify your approach," Mike emphasized. "There might be five or six things that go into hitting your driver off the tee, but you don't want to be thinking about all of those steps in a tournament. So when you say, 'Trust My Shot!' it provides a simple yet effective thought that comprises all of the key steps to success for hitting your best shot. Your phrase prompts you to move from the frustration of overthinking to a posture of trusting."

Mike paused to allow Janell time to think about what he had said – words he had spoken to thousands of athletes across all sports. He was always so interested in seeing how different athletes would apply these principles and concepts. He was especially intrigued by golfers because golf is such a mentally challenging and technical sport. While technique is important, the art of trust is essential if you truly want to play your best and unlock and unleash your talent.

Mike added, "Your other phrase 'Be Athletic' is great as well. I have seen so many golfers get so caught up in mastering their technique that they don't play loose, fierce, and free during tournaments. Being athletic involves being aware of your physical attributes, not just your technical skills. When you focus on being athletic, you bend your knees and become athletic in your stance. Your hands feel the club versus fiercely gripping the club, and the tension in your forearms dissipates as you shake your arms free before the swing. Being athletic frees up your body to accomplish what your mind just envisioned."

"I agree. So, what you're saying is that I got an 'A' on my homework!" Janell said somewhat jokingly.

"A+!" Mike replied.

"So how does all of this relate to improving my recovery time? What's so magic about a phrase and saying it before I hit my shot?" Janell asked, wanting to know more.

"Just because you say a phrase doesn't mean you will have success," Mike explained. "But it does prepare your mind and put you in a better position to be successful. Think about this scenario. You have a big shot to make, and there is water on the right side of the fairway. You look at the water, and a negative thought immediately enters your mind: 'What if I go into the water?' Or another scenario where you just hit your shot into the trees, and you begin to think about how that shot will affect your score in the future. You regret a moment you can no longer do something about.

"Your activating phrase can bring you into the current moment – the only moment that you can influence and do something about – and allow you to be present and hit your best shot," Mike continued. "Your activating phrase – 'Trust My Shot' – helps you refocus on the current moment and shot. You replace the negative thought, doubt, fear, pressure, or lack of confidence with a powerful phrase instead of trying to repress it. It's the *Law of Recency* at work."

"The Law of what?" Janell asked.

"The Law of Recency. This law, or principle, states that whatever you are thinking about 3-12 seconds before you do something impacts your performance. If you are thinking about the water – even if you say 'Don't hit into the water' or 'Avoid the water' – you are more likely to hit it into the water. Your mind hears 'WATER' very loudly and the words 'Don't' or 'Avoid' very softly. That is why trying to repress negative thoughts or words never works. You carry those thoughts into the shot, and they affect its flight.

"If, instead, you replace that thought with 'Trust My Shot!', you will carry that positive and productive thought into the shot. The positive thought now lingers in your mind for the 3-12 seconds, putting you into position to perform at your best in that moment."

Janell was intrigued by all of this. She was processing the conversation and thinking about how the idea of "recovery time" and replacing negative thoughts with positive and productive thoughts could transform not only the way she played golf but also the way she lived her life.

"When exactly do I say my phrase, and do I say it out loud?" Janell asked.

"Most of my golfers say it quietly to themselves somewhere in their pre-shot routine. You get to choose when you say it. My only rule is that you can't say it on your backswing just before your shot. At that point, you are hoping for trust instead of shooting based on trust," Mike answered.

"You're right! That would be desperation, rather than determination," Janell said.

"It's all about being present in the moment, both physically and mentally. Living in the past or future is impossible physically, but we can camp there mentally if we are not careful. I have always loved this quote from Fulton Oursler:

'Many of us crucify ourselves between two thieves - regret for the past and fear of the future.'[3]

"And these are thieves that rob us from being present in the current moment," Mike passionately explained. "This is true in golf and in life. To play at your best, you can't be thinking about what you could have done or how that moment will impact the future. When you are not fully present, you can't fully focus on what the current moment requires, which is your best," Mike added.

As they concluded this coaching session, Mike reminded Janell to:

- Be present.
- Be process-focused.
- Use her activating phrases in her pre-shot routines in practice and in her upcoming tournaments.

And his final message to her was similar to what he had encouraged her to do in other coaching sessions: "Janell, remember it's a process. Make the most of the moments in your life."

While the reminder of peak performance being a process had irritated Janell at first, she was learning to embrace, understand, and love the concept. Long-term success does not happen immediately – growth happens in the midst of many moments. It's a process!

Janell left the coffee shop excited about her renewed sense of purpose as well as about leveraging these new phrases and techniques in her practice rounds and upcoming tournaments.

The stage was set. Her next tournament was in 2 days. As Janell prepared, she worked on using her activating phrases.

She thought about how she wanted to show up to the tournament knowing confidence does not happen when you arrive or when you achieve a result. She discovered that confidence was a result of focusing on the moment and preparing your mind, spirit, and body to perform. She embraced the truth that confidence involves an inside-out approach. She learned that while confidence can be affirmed from achieving an outcome, true confidence is built and refined through preparation and hard work. She knew that her preparation was the key to stepping onto the course with belief and trust.

Janell took out the workbook Mike had given her and reviewed some final notes, including this picture:

THE IDENTITY ROLE MODEL

IF THEN... For Acceptance	BECAUSE OF... From Acceptance

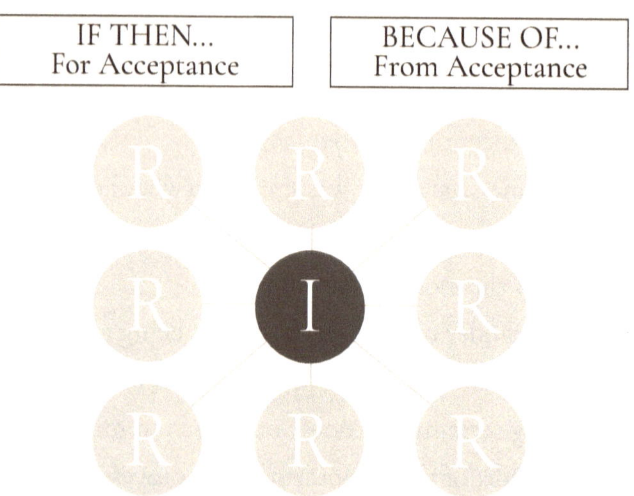

I=Identity | R=Role

As she looked at the visual, Janell remembered what they had discussed:

- Performance = Talent – Distractions.
- Your identity is not tied to your performance.
- Don't play from an IF-THEN scenario like: "If I do well or achieve an outcome, then, and only then, will I feel good about myself."
- Play from a place of acceptance instead of striving for acceptance.
- Play from a mindset of belief built on this truth: "Because Of": "Because of the preparation I have done, the work I have put in, and the belief both I and the people who support me have in me, I trust that I will play well today."
- Focus on what you can control.
- In every moment, have an "I Will" mindset.
- Be present in the moment and play shot to shot.

She was grounded, focused, and ready to compete. Janell also realized how much focusing on her *presence* – how she chose to show up to the course in terms of her demeanor, confidence, and poise – affected her *process* – how she brought her best to the moment. She understood that she could not just show up on game day and hope for a good result. She was learning how choosing the right presence, focusing on the right process, and pre-deciding how she would respond in challenging moments were the keys to performing at her best.

Janell played in a couple of tournaments before her next coaching session with Mike. She was excited to debrief how each tournament had gone and how she had applied the techniques and principles they were working on together. She also had a few questions she wanted to discuss with him about her play and the mental game. As she walked into the coffee shop, Mike was sitting in the corner where they always met.

"Janell, how are you doing?" Mike asked.

"I am doing well! We have a lot to talk about! How are you doing?"

"I am doing well! I can't wait to hear about your last few tournaments and what you have learned through those opportunities," Mike responded.

Opportunities. Mike always seemed to refer to competition as an opportunity. In fact, he used this term to describe games, matches, tests, and any other kind of performance you could think of.

Janell wondered:

"What would happen if she could fully embrace competition as an opportunity – an opportunity to compete, to unleash her talent, to encourage others, and to shine a spotlight on God, who created her and gave her the gifts and talents to play golf, lead, encourage, and serve others?"

Janell thought about opportunities she had missed in past tournaments when she had become paralyzed by the pressure of the moment. Instead of simply competing, she had focused on controlling outcomes. Instead of being faithful and giving her best, she had let the fear of failure take over her mind.

"What if I fail?" can be a haunting question that leads to disaster. "What if I succeed?" is a more constructive question, inspiring dreams that can lead to success. Competition, games, relationships, presentations, and conversations can be opportunities to use and unleash your gifts and talents if you view them in the right way and see them clearly through the lens of *opportunity*.

Janell and Mike ordered coffee and sat down to debrief the last few weeks. Mike asked her to summarize how she felt about her play, her performance, and the ways she had applied the principles they had been working on. He also asked her about her recovery time, one of the key metrics and success factors that they had focused on in their sessions. In a previous session, Mike had explained how powerful the concept of recovery time could be for Janell if she learned to embrace it and work on it.

One of the key mental game techniques is improving "recovery time," which is the ability to recover from an unexpected moment and return to the present moment. Setbacks and disappointments are a part of every game, match, performance, season, and/or career. How you respond to these setbacks will determine your growth and success as an athlete.

The best athletes and peak performers in any endeavor build resilience by improving their recovery time. This measure of an athlete's resilience is more of a qualitative value than a quantitative one. It's a skill developed over time and tested through competition. Recovery time is strengthened by using activating phrases when doubt and pressure arise and by working to stay present and process-focused.

It is so important to be aware of recovery time and how it can be an ally rather than an adversary. The quicker you recover from bad moments, the sooner you can refocus on the present and perform at your best. A quicker recovery time can give you a mental edge over your opponents which can translate into a physical edge as well. Examples of great recovery time include:

- A basketball shooter who forgets a missed shot and focuses on the next one.
- A baseball player who focuses on making a great play in the field rather than the frustration of a strikeout in the previous inning.
- A tennis player who focuses on the next point after double faulting, remembering that momentum can shift in a moment.
- An ice skater who stays in the moment and finishes strong after an early stumble in her routine.
- A volleyball team that huddles together after losing a point, refocuses to be present, and regroups poised to win the next point.

Janell loved the concept of "recovery time" and truly believed it could become the key to success to her mental game and to performing well in any situation, including making clutch putts in the moment. She also agreed with Mike that improving her recovery time should be just as important as refining the technique of her golf game.

She had been working on using her activating phrases and staying process-focused in practice and tournaments. She had also begun keeping a journal to track how well she recovered in critical moments, just as Mike had strongly encouraged her to do. She tracked her progress over time to measure the improvement in her ability to recover and to see how it helped improve her overall performance.

At the end of one coaching session, Mike asked Janell the two key questions that had become foundational to all of her tournament debriefs:

1. What did you do well?
2. What did you learn?

As Janell listened to both questions, she thought about what Mike had not asked: What did you not do well? The natural tendency was to think about strengths and weaknesses and focus on successes and failures.

As she reflected on her own past assessments and feelings about the tournaments she had played, she realized she tended to remember a few good moments and then focus on all of the things that she had not done well or could have done better. The questions she was now embracing were helping her not only learn from successful performances, but also from moments that had not gone as expected.

She was not going to dwell on the past or be discouraged by it. She was determined to use these questions to truly learn from the past – both the good and the difficult moments. She was beginning to see that all of the moments in her life could be used to mold her into who she was meant to be.

"I putted well in this tournament," Janell responded.

"That's great. Tell me more about that," Mike said.

Janell knew Mike would not settle for short phrases and one-word answers. He wanted to help her dig deeper and understand why she putted well so she could repeat that level of performance in future tournaments.

"Well, I took my time studying the line of the putt," Janell continued. "I visualized the path of the putt, the break of the ball, and saw the ball going in every time. Then I chose to trust my vision and executed the shot. Picture it, paint it!"

Janell remembered the story Mike had told her about his mentor, David Cook, who told him about Johnny, the teaching professional at the club where David had worked and played as a boy. Johnny became a mentor to David and frequently talked about artistry on the golf course. He often shouted "Picaso!" after hitting the golf ball, explaining that he was signing his shot like an artist.

Mike had reminded Janell that she needed to be an artist on the golf course. Picture your shots. Paint your shots. Visualize the shot. Hit the shot. And as David said, "See it. Feel it. Trust it."

Mike loved hearing Janell repeat what they were working on. "That's right! Picture it. Paint it! It's so simple."

"What else did you do well?" Mike asked.

Janell knew Mike would not settle for talking about only one good thing from her tournaments, so she shared other key moments that had gone well such as how she could feel her recovery time improving and how she was implementing more of the principles they were working on together.

Janell was excited about this moment in time and the opportunities her junior year presented. She was beginning to grasp the purpose for which she was created. God had given Janell specific gifts and talents, and she felt closest to God when she used them to honor Him. She was keeping in step with His Spirit as she walked along a purposeful path.

Janell was embracing all of the moments in her life – her past and present, her successes and setbacks, and her wins and her losses. As Tyler Perry once said, "If you begin to realize that every moment in your life happened for the greater good of who you are...it can really elevate you and change your whole trajectory."[4]

Janell understood the power of this perspective and the clarity of her calling in life, which was way beyond golf!

But the true test of her perseverance was just around the corner.

Breakthrough With The Boys

"Coach JJ, how did you recover from bad shots? Sometimes, I let those moments get in my head and keep me from being present for the next shot," Lane said.

"Yeah, that happens to me too!" Braden added.

While Janell had worked with many girls as a part of JJ's Juniors, she also coached many boys who were aspiring golfers. Lane and Braden were two of her best students.

"'That's a great question! And as my mental coach told me repeatedly, it's a process. The key is that you can't let one bad moment dominate your thinking or define your identity. Both of you are very good golfers, and you have the talent and drive to become great. I learned from working with my mental performance coach that golf becomes simpler and more fun when you play it one shot at a time. It's like that in life too. If we worry about the past or fear the future, we will never be present and enjoy this moment called today," Janell responded.

"Did you ever deal with doubt or negative thoughts?" Braden asked.

"Yes, definitely!" Janell quickly answered. "But I learned how to deal with doubt and choose faith over fear, even in the big moments."

"How did you do that?" Lane asked.

"I learned to play with joy and focus," Janell said.

"Tell us more about that," Braden said.

"My mental coach taught me that it is possible to play with joy and focus. Many people think that to be focused, you have to be stressed and looked stressed. Mike taught me that you can play with joy and focus at the same time. You can smile and enjoy the scenery of the course while still focusing on hitting an approach shot three to four feet from the hole. In fact, he emphasized that if I wanted to play at my best and truly unleash my talent, joy had to be a part of it. Think about how much time you invest practicing and playing golf."

"Yeah, it's a lot of hours!" Lane jumped in.

"It is. And the tournaments that you play in last a long time," Janell added. "It's hard to be focused for four to five hours straight, so you have to find joy in the in-between moments – the moments between a great drive and walking up to hit your next shot, the moments when you walk to the green to finish a hole, admiring the trees and the layout of the course along the way. When you play with joy and focus, you will have a lot more fun, and you will play your best golf."

"That makes sense," Lane and Braden said in unison.

"Are you going to watch the game this weekend?" Lane asked. "Your team is going down!"

"No way!" Janell replied. "Do you really think that Alabama can beat my Aggies? How about this – if your team wins, I will get you some snacks from the club snack bar. But if my Texas A&M Aggies win, you both have to do extra golf drills. Deal?"

"Deal!" Lane and Braden said.

"You'd better get those snacks ready!" Braden added.

"You'd better be prepared to do extra work on Monday!" Janell said with a confident grin.

"We will see. Hey, Coach JJ, we have one more question. Which year of high school was the most fun for you? Which was your best year, and which one are you most proud of?" Lane asked.

"They were all great and full of many memories and moments," Janell answered. Upon thinking a little more, she said, "If I had to pick just one, it might be my senior year. That was the moment I learned what I really had inside of me."

CHAPTER 8

Janell's Senior Year

Janell's junior year flew by. She was voted Team Captain of her golf team for the third year in a row reflecting not only her talent but also her leadership. She was the best player and a respected leader – an uncommon combination for the captain of any team. She was also selected District MVP for the third year in a row, highlighting her dominance and consistency of play. Her peers – both teammates and competitors – respected and appreciated her, which showed the impact she was having on others through the platform golf gave her.

Although things were going well, she had still not received any college scholarships. Some schools had shown interest, but none had made a formal offer yet. Janell knew that life was not all about getting the big offer, and she had learned to place her identity in something bigger than a golf score or the approval of others, including a college or university. She was also beginning to wonder whether she even wanted to play at the next level. She believed she could, but she was not yet sure if that was the plan God had in store for her.

Janell's favorite Bible verse was Proverbs 4:26 (ESV) –

"Ponder the path of your feet; then all your ways will be sure."

She had this verse prominently placed on her varsity letter jacket, which she carried with her to school most days so she would not get cold in class. While many of her peers covered their jackets with patches of honors and accomplishments, she chose her favorite Bible verse to glorify God, who had given her the ability to accomplish those achievements.

She was walking with the Creator and Author of her life, carefully considering each step to make sure she was traveling the right path. She recognized how easy it was to focus on yourself rather than God. In every aspect of her life, she was learning to release fear and doubt and embrace faith and trust. The journey mattered as much as the destination!

In preparation for her senior year, Janell played in some summer tournaments. She wanted to make the most of the season, and she felt both excited and cautiously optimistic it would be an awesome finale to her high school journey. As the last few weeks of summer passed, she reflected on 2 questions:

1. Had she made the most of her moments so far?
2. What would the final year of high school be like?

A week before her senior year started, Janell met with Mike at the local golf course where they had worked together so many times before on her mental game. As she walked up to the clubhouse, Janell saw Mike on the putting green.

"Hi Janell," Mike said.

"Hello Mike. How are you doing?"

"I am doing great. How are you doing is the real question? Senior year! Are you excited?"

"Definitely! I am so looking forward to this opportunity!" Janell said with enthusiasm.

"Are you ready to get started?" Mike asked.

"Absolutely!" Janell responded.

"Today, we are going to play several holes and work on building consistency in your pre-shot routine as well as using your trust and activating phrases," Mike explained. "I also want us to focus on responding rather than reacting. My goal is to help you have your best year yet!"

"Sounds great! I am ready," Janell responded.

Janell and Mike got in the golf cart and drove to the first tee. Janell greeted the starter, whom she had gotten to know well after countless practice sessions and rounds on her home course.

"Hello, Janell! Practice session today? I see you brought your sidekick with you," the starter said.

"Yes, we are going to play a few holes and work on a few things to improve my golf game. How are you doing?" Janell replied.

"I am doing well. It's not too crowded out there today, so you should be good to go." Then the starter turned to Mike and added, "That young lady has one of the best swings I have ever seen and one of the sweetest spirits you will ever find."

"Totally agree on both counts," Mike said.

Janell smiled and responded, "Ya'll are too kind!"

Her interactions with others were consistently thoughtful and encouraging. She measured her words and considered her ways as a means to encourage people and point them to Jesus, the true source of her strength and peace. In a world so often marked by hurt and division, she was a light in the darkness.

Janell drove up to the tee box and hit her first shot. Over the next few holes, she and Mike worked on mental game techniques she was learning to implement and master. Visualize the shot. Be consistent in the pre-shot routine. Get a great feel for the shot. Trust your shot!

For each shot, Janell divided the approach into two metaphorical boxes: the Think Box and the Play Box. The Think Box was for observation and strategy. Mike had always encouraged her to take in the whole picture and observe her surroundings including the hole's layout. He had reminded her that the designers of golf courses try to get you to focus on the distractions such as sand, water, and trees to create fear and doubt.

Observation allows you to constructively process the information. The strategy step of the Think Box allows you to develop a plan to reach the target based on the information you observed. The goal is to visualize and seek the target rather than avoid the obstacles.

Janell had recalled the axiom Mike had repeated so often during their time together:

What you choose to focus on magnifies in size

She knew if she focused on them, the distractions would become bigger in her mind. She had learned that when she said phrases like "I am just going to avoid the sand," her mind would hear the word "Avoid" very softly and the word "Sand" very loudly. Janell wanted to focus on the target...both in golf and in life!

The Play Box was where Janell put it all together once she had thought about the shot she wanted to make. It was the place where she trusted her preparation and allowed her abilities to take over, allowing belief and faith to overcome doubt and fear. Trust is an incredible place where doubt gives way to belief and fear submits to faith. And on the golf course and in life, it is a zone where we all desire to be!

As they prepared to tee off on the 5th hole, Mike went through the same routine they had used and practiced on every other hole to help her focus on observing and then developing the proper strategy.

"Janell, what do you see?" Mike asked.

"I see trees on the left and sand on the right and water in front of the hole in the distance," Janell observed.

"Ok, now walk me through your shot. Picture it," Mike encouraged.

"I am going to hit a left to right shot about medium height, and I see it landing in the fairway near the sand about 150 yards from the hole," Janell answered.

"Ok, you pictured it. Now, go paint it," which was Mike's way of saying "Trust it!"

After Janell went through her pre-shot routine, she decisively stepped in to her "play box" – the place she consistently excelled. She didn't push or press her swing and rarely changed her mechanics to hit a bigger shot. Instead, she focused on the same tempo that had become a part of not only her golf swing but also her life.

The right rhythm is needed in all parts of life. Great dancers use rhythm and tempo to move to the beat at the appropriate pace. Rhythm and timing are also important in sports, including golf, where a swing is perfected over many hours of practice and executed with precision and timing in tournament moments. And rhythm is important in life, where peace, growth, and balance are essential to becoming present in the moments of your life. You must be aware of the importance of rhythm in your life. Rhythm creates the structure, and timing and tempo make it work.

As Janell hit her shot, the ball flew off the club, making a beautiful sound and landing just a couple of feet from where she had envisioned it. She smiled as Mike just shook his head in amazement, saying loud enough for her and everyone else on the adjacent holes to hear, "That's awesome! You see, Janell, golf's not that hard when you hit shots like that."

As they walked to the next shot, they discussed the sport of golf and how it was a great metaphor for life. Janell had played many sports, but she eventually chose golf because she wanted full responsibility for the impact of her actions. She looked forward to not having to depend on anyone else but herself in the heat of competition. She enjoyed the challenge and the opportunity.

Janell had a natural swing that she had worked hard to perfect and make it look effortless. Each incredible shot represented countless hours of purposeful repetition and practice.

As Janell prepared for the next shot, she suddenly looked perplexed as she analyzed the yardage and club choice.

Mike asked, "What's wrong?"

"Well, this shot requires my 5-iron," Janell answered.

"And?" Mike asked.

"And I typically hit my 5-iron well, but lately I have struggled with the 5-iron and in my last tournament there were a couple of holes where I did not hit that club well, so I am not too sure about my 5-iron right now and not sure if I want to use it for this shot."

Mike looked at her also perplexed, but for a different reason. He did not know if it was because he had just heard one of the longest run-on sentences without a pause or punctuation in the history of the world or if it was because he could not believe Janell would even have these thoughts after the incredible tee shot she just hit moments before.

Performance can be a peculiar mystery, full of twists and turns. Just when you begin to feel confident, one poor shot, one unexpected setback, or one moment of doubt can make you question everything. You become unsure of the journey you are on and begin to question your next step on the path. The key is to keep moving forward – one step at a time and one moment at a time.

Mike looked back at the tee box for a couple of seconds, and then down at the ball. He did this twice, then looked at the target ahead before returning his gaze to the ball as he considered his next words.

After a moment, he asked, "Janell, what was the first part of that paragraph that you just shared – the thing you said right at the beginning?"

"I typically hit my 5-iron well," Janell said with a bit of reluctance.

Mike immediately intervened stopping her from uttering one more word and said in a most decisive voice, "PERIOD! Then go hit that shot!"

Janell looked at him shocked. Although he hadn't yelled, Mike had never been this forceful about a point or really anything they had ever talked about.

She was ready with club in hand to step up to the ball, knowing the shot she wanted to hit. She swung the club, and the ball flew as if it was destined for a locked-in target. It landed on the green just past the hole, spinning back and stopping about 2-3 feet from the hole.

Janell looked back at Mike in amazement, and Mike just shook his head and laughed. He knew he had taken a risk by being so forceful to predict a shot that he knew Janell could make, but not certain because of her initial doubt that she would make.

"You see Janell, it's tempting to put commas where a period should be. Commas lead to a long list of excuses of why you cannot do something or create doubt. Periods end the sentence, leaving you no other choice but to trust."

Janell and Mike drove to the green, and Janell tapped in her putt to make a birdie. As she picked up the ball out of the cup, she looked back in amazement at what just happened.

This was a moment that Janell would never forget and that would strengthen and sustain her in future moments. While she didn't know what was waiting for her around the corner, she knew she had just experienced a breakthrough lesson about trust, perseverance, resiliency, and the power of positive self-talk.

They finished a few more holes continuing to work on consistency in her process and trust in her approach. As the coaching session ended and they arrived at the clubhouse, Janell saw a few of the patrons that regularly played at the golf course, friends of her family who often played with Janell's dad and younger brother.

One of the men yelled out to Janell, "Working on your mental game, I see," noticing who was with her. "Maybe, I need a mental coach!"

Janell wasn't sure if the man was joking or serious but responded confidently, "I have seen your game, and I am sure Mike could help you lower your score."

The other men at the table laughed, and the man who had spoken admitted, "You're probably right. Golf is a mental game!"

Janell and Mike drove to the parking lot to drop off her clubs, and Mike left her with this thought: "Janell, trust is a choice. It is something that you can choose to do...or not. I love Proverbs 3:5-6 (ESV), which says:

⁵Trust in the Lord with all your heart,
　and do not lean on your own understanding.
⁶ In all your ways acknowledge him,
　and he will make straight your paths.'

"When you trust in God in all things with all your heart, He will guide you down the right path," Mike continued. "Don't ever forget that! And don't ever let the fear of the moment overtake you. You proved today that you can overcome any fear or negative thought."

Mike gave her a fist bump, got in his car, and drove off. Janell stood by her car in the parking lot and reflected on what she had learned today. She thought about how anyone can struggle with doubt – including her. But she also realized that she had a choice: she could choose trust instead. She could choose faith over fear. She went back to the clubhouse, opened her journal, and wrote the word "TRUST" in capital letters in her journal entry for the day.

Janell's senior year flew by, and she made the most of it both on and off the course. She went to football games. She hung out with friends. She studied and did her best in the classroom. She served in her school's community service programs. She was making the most of her moments.

People of all ages gravitated toward her because of her caring and empathetic spirit and magnetic personality. In a culture that can be cruel and divisive, Janell was compassionate and devoted. She was a loyal friend who brought the best out in others. Her presence preceded her impact.

Janell's empathy and caring spirit was born out of suffering. When Janell was around 10 years old, she went in for a routine physical that spiraled into months of 24-hour urine collections, endless vials of blood work, and many trips to Texas Children's Hospital. Her condition was a medical paradox. She felt fine on the outside while inside a disease that the doctors could not diagnose was waging a stage 4 war on her kidneys.

The transition from a healthy child who did not know how to swallow a pill to a patient facing the possibility of a kidney transplant was extremely jarring to her. Since no one could properly define what was happening, she named this illness "Janell's Disease." Still in elementary school, Janell turned 11 the week before the biopsy. As she and her family waited for the test results, Janell asked her mom if she was going to die – an unimaginably heartbreaking question to hear from your 11-year old daughter.

Based on the test results, a team of doctors from multiple specialties agreed Janell needed to begin a high dose of steroids immediately and if her condition did not improve, chemotherapy would be the next step. When the steroids began, the "invisible" battle finally became visible. The medication caused a puffy face and other physical changes that she had to carry into the vulnerable halls of junior high. For the first time, Janell felt the sting of being judged by people who didn't know her before this happened and could not see what was happening inside her body.

The most profound moment of this part of her journey did not happen in a lab or during a kidney biopsy; it happened in the quiet, shared space of a waiting room when she was 11. Surrounded by children whose illnesses were unmistakable — kids in wheelchairs, others without hair, and some tethered to IV poles — Janell saw a reflection of her own hidden reality. She turned to her mother and spoke a truth that would become a defining moment in her life and shape her compassion for others:

"You never know what someone is going through in their life. You see these kids who are obviously sick, and here I am looking and feeling fine; yet I'm here seeing specialists for something they don't even have a name for."

In that moment, Janell realized that pain and struggle are not always loud or visible.

The medicine she was taking gradually improved her condition, and over time the dosage was reduced. The monthly doctor visits and the

24-hour urine collections continued, but by the end of the year, she was off the steroid after eight-months of taking the medication. Slowly, her body began to return to her normal appearance. Her appointments became less frequent, and when she turned 18, she was released from treatment at Texas Children's Hospital.

This season of life did more than teach her how to be a patient. It taught her that every person carries burdens the world cannot see. In the midst of children facing dire diagnoses and the uncertainty of her own future, Janell's heart was permanently softened. Janell chose to turn her suffering – her "moment" – into a lifelong mission to care for the hidden hurts of others.

In her senior year, district play began. Janell was again selected as the Team Captain for her golf team, marking the fourth year that she would serve as the team's leader. She knew this team had the potential to do well, and she was determined to play her best and help others do the same.

She also supported her friends in other sports including the girls' soccer team. Having grown up playing alongside many of them, she enjoyed cheering them on as they won big games and achieved success in the playoffs. Even in the midst of her busy schedule, she made time to encourage them, attend games, and even share some of the lessons and principles that she had learned from Mike.

She also was given opportunities to share what she was learning on bigger stages.

"You ready?" Mike asked as Janell walked through the door to the classroom where she had sat in history class just a few hours earlier.

"Yes, I am ready. But are you ready? That is the real question," Janell replied with a hint of confidence.

Janell's dad, Chuck, was president of the high school athletics booster club and had invited Mike to speak to the parents of the school's athletes about developing resilience and mental toughness. Mike asked Janell to be a part of this presentation and share what she had learned.

"Yes, I am ready, and I am excited about this moment. Just think – you didn't want to meet with me at first, and now we are giving presentations together as you share all the great things you've learned. What a transformation," Mike said with a smile.

"Well, I'm your best student, so you're very fortunate!" Janell responded.

"Yes, you are," Mike said. "And this is a great opportunity for the student to become the teacher."

At that moment, Janell's dad entered the classroom. "Hello, Mike. Hi, Janell. Are ya'll ready?" Chuck asked.

"Yes!" Janell and Mike said in unison.

"Well, we should have a great group tonight, and they're excited to hear what you have to say," Chuck continued.

As parents began entering the classroom and Janell greeted them, Chuck pulled Mike aside and said, "I just want to thank you for what you have done for Janell. Donna and I are so grateful! She has learned so much from you, and we have seen tremendous growth in her mental game over the last two years."

"Thanks Chuck!" Mike responded. "I'm the one who is grateful for the opportunity. Janell is an exceptional person and leader, not to mention one of the best athletes I have ever worked with. I simply shared a few principles and asked the right questions to help her unlock what was already inside of her."

"Yeah, she's special," Chuck said proudly.

More parents entered the room, and Chuck welcomed everyone, covered some announcements for the parents, and then introduced Mike.

Mike had already worked with other athletes and teams at the high school, and because some of his sons were beginning to attend there as well, he knew many of the parents in the room.

As Mike began to speak, he shared how he had stepped into the journey of helping athletes, the people who had invested in him and encouraged him along the way, and why developing and nurturing the mental health of the next generation of leaders mattered so deeply to him. He spoke about how sports had always played a significant role in his life, then shared this quote:

"Sports should not be a place where we find anxiety and angst. It should be a place where we discover grit, growth, and greatness!"

Mike knew from his experience that many of the sons and daughters represented in the room were experiencing things like fear and deep anxiety driven by the pressure to perform and the cost of comparison. In the age of social media, he knew that the athletes and students he had worked with could scroll on their phones and see the best moments of everyone else's lives and compare them with their worst moments. They could easily fall into the trap of thinking that everyone else was living their best life.

As he continued, Mike spoke about joy and focus and how both could coexist in competition. In fact, he said that joy was just as important as focus and essential to performing at your best, unlocking your talent, and playing loose, fierce, and free.

Finally, Mike shared the "5 Keys to a Championship Mindset" – the same five keys that he had taught so many other coaches, teams, and athletes, including Janell. He also shared and explained the *top ten* list of ways to build and nurture confidence in your athlete:

As he finished this part of the presentation, he introduced Janell and invited her to share her perspective on performance and how these principles were helping her both as an athlete and a person.

KEYS TO BUILDING CONFIDENCE IN YOUR ATHLETE

- Communicate feedback in terms of their "potential to be."

- Positive/constructive feedback ratio 5:1.

- Give feedback about their behavior, not their identity.

- Praise progress…toward a goal or outcome (Growth Mindset).

- Don't use words like "always" or "never."

- Build up vs. tear down.

- Facilitate productive conversations…with every stakeholder involved in their growth.

- On game day, simplify.

- Sometimes, just enjoy the silence and listen.

- Give freedom to innovate and learn from their mistakes.

"Hello, everyone," Janell began. "I know most of ya'll, but I am Janell Lysack, and I am a senior and a golfer at Seven Lakes. Mike and I have worked together for the past two years, and I have learned so much during this time. The principles that Mike shared are the same ones we have been working on. At first, I didn't want to meet with him – not because he wasn't a nice person, but because I didn't think I needed to meet with a mental performance coach or work on my mental game. I thought that if I just continued hitting golf balls on the range, I would improve, and that any regret I had over missed putts and opportunities would eventually fade. I learned that I was wrong about that. I learned that working on your mental game – in golf and in life – is one of the best things you can do to unlock and unleash your true potential!"

Janell shared a few more things about how she learned to apply the five keys, how improving her recovery time had helped her to play her best, and how developing and following a consistent routine had set her up for success both on and off the course.

As she concluded, Chuck asked whether the parents had any questions for Janell and Mike. A man in the back spoke up and said, "That was a great presentation, and we appreciate both of you sharing this information. Janell, it sounds like you know this stuff pretty well. I'm wondering: what do we need him for?" he asked, jokingly pointing to Mike.

The whole room laughed, and Mike immediately responded, "You're right! She's an expert!"

The goal of leadership is to invest in the life of another person. It is not to gather followers or tell people what to do. It is to teach others how to lead, to share information and insights, to reveal experience and lessons learned, and to ask the kind of questions that lead to the best answers – the answers that lead to excellence and to a life of true significance.

Mike believed knowledge and wisdom are meant to be shared, not hoarded, so that is what he did with Janell and so many other athletes. Now Janell was learning to demonstrate the art of servant leadership by sharing the lessons she had learned. As she took what she had been taught and made it her own, she was able not only to perform at her best, but also to inspire and teach others to do the same. She was discovering that helping others succeed and making a positive impact in their lives was what she was made to do.

Everyone left the classroom reflecting on the different parts of the presentation that had resonated with them. As Chuck walked out with Janell and Mike, he said, "Well, that was a great moment, right Mike?"

"Yes, it was," Mike replied. "Thanks for putting this together."

"I'll see you at home," Chuck said to Janell as he kissed her on her forehead and got in his car.

"You did great!" Mike said to Janell. "And there will be many more moments for you to share with and invest in others. I have always thought that the biggest 'thank you' I could give to my mentors was to share with others what they invested in me. And that is exactly what I am doing. Janell, that is the biggest 'thank you' you can give to me, too!"

"That's a great perspective," Janell said, and they both got in their cars and left.

And Mike was right. A few weeks later, he received an invitation to speak at a prestigious country club and spa, and he asked Janell to join him. It was a wonderful opportunity, and this time Mike divided the presentation, allowing Janell to teach half of it to the audience, which included top business leaders and entrepreneurs, aspiring professional tennis players, and two men's collegiate golf teams with their coaches.

Janell did an incredible job of explaining how these mental game principles had become the key to her success on and off the course. She was also growing more comfortable speaking to larger groups and stepping into leadership roles that would serve her well in the future.

Growth is a process. Leadership expert and author John Maxwell was once asked: "Are leaders born or are they made?" His response: "Yes!" Leaders are born with gifts, AND they are refined through a process of personal growth. Great leaders recognize and seize these moments as opportunities to become their best. This is exactly what Janell was doing. God created her with unique gifts and talents, and she was learning to recognize those opportunities and steward those gifts for His glory.

Investing in the Next Generation

"You didn't bring a coat?! Again?" Janell asked, looking genuinely puzzled.

"I forgot," Reagan answered.

"Hold on and never fear – Coach JJ is here!"

Janell went to her car and returned to the practice range with a jacket bearing a Texas A&M logo, which she handed to Reagan.

"I know you're not an Aggie, but you can be today and represent the best university," Janell said confidently.

"Thanks, Coach JJ! What are we working on today?" Reagan asked curiously.

"We're working on your mental game," Janell answered.

"My mental game? I thought we were going to play a few holes and work on my drives and short game," Reagan replied puzzled.

"We are," Janell said. "But as we go, I want to help you understand some principles that will help you not only in golf but also in life. I was fortunate to have someone invest in me, and the biggest 'thank you' I could give him is to invest in others, including you, and share that same wisdom. You see, golf is not just trying to hit a tiny ball across a scenic fairway and eventually into a cup with a flag and pole sticking out of it. It also involves developing resilience along the way, especially when things don't go right – when you don't hit it well, when you miss a putt, and when the score of the day is not in your favor.

"Golf is a mental game," Janell continued. "And I want you to be strong in every moment and have true faith in the midst of fear."

"That sounds great to me," Reagan said with a smile.

Janell saw herself in all of the young juniors she was coaching at Hermitage Golf Course, especially the girls. She wanted them to know the power of a resilient mindset paired with the joy of playing a game they loved. She wanted these young golfers to know God had created them with gifts and talents for a purpose. She wanted to serve as a role model for what's possible when you fully embrace and engage in the moments of your life.

Reagan and Coach JJ spent the rest of the day talking about the 5 keys to a championship mindset, playing a few holes, and competing against each other. Janell liked to make these sessions fun, and she often set up contests to see if her students could beat her. One of these contests involved trying to hit the 100-yard sign. Her students quickly realized that Coach JJ was not going to just let them win. She played to win, which was a great reminder to Reagan and the rest of JJ's Juniors to always give your best.

As they finished the last hole, Janell said to Reagan, "Reagan, you have a lot of talent, and God has blessed you with leadership skills and a humble, yet confident spirit. I know you are going to do great things – in golf and in life. Make it count. Make the most of your moments."

"I will!" Reagan responded with a grateful smile. "And I am looking to forward to my moments and opportunities. Thanks so much for all that you have done for me and for serving as a role model to me."

As they walked back to the clubhouse, they debriefed about the day, including what was shared and learned. Once at the clubhouse, they sat down to eat some food.

Reagan turned to Janell to ask one final question. "Coach JJ, what was the hardest moment you ever had to face as a golfer?"

"Well, Reagan. That was during my senior year," Janell responded as she returned to sharing her journey.

CHAPTER 9
A Crucible Moment

"Peace I leave with you; my peace I give you. I do not give to you as the world gives. Do not let your hearts be troubled and do not be afraid."

JOHN 14:27

The regular golf season was a success for both Janell and her high school team. They were approaching the district tournament with tremendous momentum. Everything was unfolding just as she had envisioned. Janell even had a date to the Senior Prom, which was still several weeks away. Her "date" was simply a friend who had asked her, and she was looking forward to spending time with a group of friends and topping off an incredible senior year.

Then tragedy suddenly struck! Janell's prom date died in a tragic accident, and in an instance, everything seemed horrific. Janell, along with her friends, began wrestling with the questions that arise in moments like these. Why did this person have to die? Why did he die so young? Where was God in all of this? What am I supposed to feel, say, or do? Life seemed unbearable.

She was engulfed in a fog of despair and did not know how to find her way out. Her compassionate, caring, and empathetic spirit was weighed down by a cloud of "Whys?" and "What ifs?" With the district tournament – Janell's big moment – just a few days away, she neither desired nor was in the proper state of mind to play. She felt lost.

Janell's mom called Mike and said, "Janell needs some counseling from you. In fact, we may all need some counseling!"

She proceeded to tell Mike about the death of Janell's friend and the toll it was taking on her. While Janell had not known this person for very long, the depth of her friendships began the moment she met people. She was the kind of person who never met a person she didn't like, and she was so consistently kind, caring, and compassionate to others. She was the kind of friend everyone wanted. Janell was everyone's best friend!

Mike drove to Janell's house not knowing what to expect. The street outside her house was lined with cars.

Janell's mom greeted Mike at the door and said, "She is very down. I have never seen her like this. Her friends are upstairs trying to get her to talk. I just want you to know that she may not be able to talk about this, but I know your presence here will mean a great deal to her in this moment."

"Thank you, Donna. I am so sorry this has happened. How is the boy's family doing? Have you spoken to them?" Mike asked.

"They are doing okay. As you can imagine, they are heartbroken and grieving his death."

Donna let Mike inside, and he immediately greeted Janell's father with a handshake and hug. Mike then walked upstairs and found a room full of friends consoling a very distraught girl in the corner of her room. As he entered, Janell's friends stepped back allowing him to see her. She looked as though she had been crying for days, and her face wore the weight of grief. Golf was the furthest thing from her mind as she mourned the loss of a friend.

"Hi, Janell. I am so sorry this has happened. How are you doing?" Mike asked, unsure if this was the right question and trying to balance speaking, listening, and simply being present. In moments like these, it is so hard to know what to say or do.

Janell did not immediately answer. The weight of the situation was more than she could bear, and words failed her. The person who had always seemed to know what to say and how to uplift the spirits of others now sat motionless on the floor of her room with a hollow look on her face.

Mike continued, almost trying to fill the void in both the conversation and her heart. "I am not going to say too much in this moment, but I do want you to know I am here. We are all here for you. We are praying for the family of this young man, and we are praying for you. I will be here when you are ready to talk, just as I have always been."

Mike lingered a few more minutes, though they felt like hours, and then started toward the door. A crowd of friends had quietly watched the exchange. From the corner of the room, a small, hoarse voice said, "Mike...thanks. Thanks for everything."

Mike turned and saw a face trying to smile, but still struggling under the weight of the moment. He turned to Janell and repeated, "I am here. We are all here for you," before walking out of the room.

Mike walked back downstairs as Janell's friends came back into the room to try and console Janell.

"This is bad," Janell's mom said. "It's bad for everyone involved, especially this young man and his family. We are praying for them and can only imagine how they are feeling with the loss of their son at such a young age. I have never seen Janell so distraught. She doesn't even seem like herself."

"I know," Mike responded. "She had this hollow look on her face, as though you could see right through her."

"And while we don't want to think about this because life is so much more important than sports, the district tournament is only a couple of days away, and she is already saying she doesn't want to play. Mike, I don't know what we are going to do. How do we navigate something like this? What is the right thing to do?"

Donna was asking the questions that we were all thinking but were too scared to mention. This moment was messing up the other moments that we had been planning for. Things had been going so smoothly, and then life – and in this case death – got in the way.

What is the right response to a situation like this? How do you move on when grief seems to be the only appropriate response? How much space and time do you give grief? And do you move *past it* or *through it*, hoping to find purpose, clarity, and peace in the process? Answers to these questions would be revealed in the days to come including whether Janell would play in the biggest tournament of her life so far?

The next 48 hours would be among the most intense of her life. The only thing that felt real to Janell in that moment was that someone she knew with so much life ahead of him was gone. Everything else seemed irrelevant, or so she thought.

When someone dies, a flood of emotions and thoughts can follow. Responses can range from anger about what happened to disappointment about whether we made the most of our moments with them while they were alive. Often, we question the future because we lack clarity to move forward. They say that grief takes time, but how much time is enough? And when, if ever, will we begin to feel whole again?

Janell did not want to "get over" this moment. To her, getting over the death of her friend felt like forgetting it had ever happened. It is hard to know how long you should grieve, and she was not wanting to give up this feeling anytime soon. And as Monday approached, she would have to decide whether she would play in the district tournament on Tuesday. The questions of "Would she? Could she? And should she play?" weighed heavy on her heart and mind.

Monday came, and the school day felt like a blur to Janell. She struggled to focus and did not know what she should be feeling. She was also anticipating her upcoming meeting with Mike. What would he say? What could he say in a moment like this? Would he try and convince her to play in the tournament? How would or should she respond?

Her thoughts swirled as she drove to her home course clubhouse. Janell parked the car and slowly walked inside. She was not there to practice. She went straight to the dining area, which had been full of people earlier but was now as desolate as she felt.

Mike arrived and walked inside to find Janell at a big circular table. He put his journal down on the table and sat down. At first, no greetings or words were exchanged. Finally, he broke the silence with the obvious question, "How are you doing?"

"I am doing okay," Janell replied almost mechanically.

"Well, okay seems better than how you were yesterday," Mike said carefully. "Can we talk about your thoughts and feelings about tomorrow?"

By this point in their coaching relationship, Mike had earned a place at the table to help Janell in a wide range of situations. They had been working together for over two years through a variety of moments. Successful tournaments. Individual and team accomplishments. Setbacks and losses. But this would be the hardest challenge they had faced together, and it was far bigger than a golf score.

"I am not sure," was all Janell could manage in that moment.

"You're not sure about playing, or you're not sure about your feelings?" Mike asked gently.

"Both," Janell breathed.

"Then, let's talk about both," Mike said. "First, tell me what you are thinking and feeling."

Janell was not sure she could articulate what she was feeling or thinking. While she appreciated the question, she was unsure how to answer.

After what felt like an hour, Janell finally admitted, "I just don't know if I can or should do it. Going out to play a game now feels trivial and uncaring."

Mike listened with care and concern. In moments like these, no one knows exactly what to say but being present and listening with an empathetic heart is a good place to start. He could see on her face and sense the anguish she felt and the anxiety she was carrying. He also saw the caring spirit that loved others – one of the incredible qualities God had given her that only grew stronger with age and wisdom.

"I don't know why this happened," Janell continued. "He was so young with a lot of life left to live. Where is God in all of this?"

Janell was finally able to put into words what so many people hold inside when it comes to grief. Cognitive Neuroscientist and Communication Pathologist Dr. Caroline Leaf says the following:

"Dealing with loss and the grief that comes with this feeling often means facing something that is both final and unchangeable, which makes grief very hard to manage. And, contrary to popular opinion, time doesn't just 'heal' this feeling of loss. Rather, time helps to create the space necessary to come to terms with the inevitability of the loss."[1]

Janell was facing something that was final and unchangeable. Her caring heart and fighter's spirit were wrestling to accept this loss and the reality that there was nothing she could do about it.

"I can't explain *Why* this happened, nor can I make the feelings of loss and pain go away," Mike responded. "But, I can offer you a few questions to reflect on as you process your feelings, gather your thoughts, and consider your next move."

Louie Giglio offers four questions to help in times of loss and grief providing a more productive path.[2] Instead of repeatedly asking "Why?" – the one question we often stumble over, demanding answers from God and others – Louie suggests asking God more constructive questions:

1. What do You want to do in me?
2. What do You want to do through me?
3. Who do You want me to meet?
4. How can You be glorified?

Louie had been a mentor to Mike at Baylor and greatly influenced him. As a college student, Mike attended Louie's Bible Study called *Choice*, which ministered to thousands of students who were seeking to grow spiritually during a pivotal season of their lives. Eventually, Louie and his wife, Shelley, moved to Atlanta and founded a global ministry called *Passion*.

The "Life Interrupted" series, along with many of Louie's other talks over the years had deeply impacted Mike. His own life had been "interrupted" at the age of five when his father left their family, forcing his mom to pick up the pieces and walk through the pain of divorce. It was only through the strength and power of Jesus that Mike and his mom were able to leverage this moment in a way that glorified God and strengthened their faith and resolve. Now, it was time to share these questions in hopes of helping a high school senior do the same thing.

Mike shared his story, including the departure of his dad, the faith of his mom, and the impact of his grandfather and the many other male role models in his life including his high school basketball coach and Louie Giglio. He also compassionately shared the four questions with Janell – questions that had helped him so much.

In moments like this, we can easily switch into "fix-it" mode offering three or four steps to a solution in a way that leaves no room to process the pain. We say things like, "Just do these things, and you will be fine." But in times of grief, the path must be discovered, and it often takes time to embrace a new way of thinking before a new way of living can begin.

The day wore on as they talked through the grief of the moment and the impact it could have on one of the most important decisions Janell had ever faced: to play or not to play. That was the question before her. What would she decide to do?

Moments with Meredith

"That must have been very difficult!" Meredith said to Coach JJ. What were you thinking? What were you feeling?"

"It was hard. I felt for my friend and his family. Tragedy put golf in its proper perspective, and at that moment, I didn't feel like playing at all. Yet, I had been working all year for the opportunity to play and lead our team to victory in the district tournament. I had a 48-hour window to make a crucial decision."

"What did you decide to do?" Meredith asked.

"How I decided is just as important to understand as what I decided to do," Janell responded. "You see, Meredith, life is full of choices just like golf. When you are playing a round, you are faced with all kinds of choices about your shot including the thoughts you are thinking, the club you will use, and the type of shot you will hit. You must observe and be aware of the variables and circumstances while remaining focused on and trusting your preparation and the principles that guide your best golf and also your best life."

"You're right, Coach JJ," Meredith responded. "And every time we step onto the course, I learn so much more than how to play my best golf. The things you teach me apply to life as well."

"That's right, and a wise mentor once reminded me of that," Janell confirmed.

"So how did you make the decision?" Meredith continued. "And I still want to know if you decided to play?"

"Well, Mike gave me some questions to consider. What would my friend want me to do? And more importantly, how can God be glorified in and through this moment? I also realized that the principles and mental performance techniques that I had learned had prepared me for moments like this one. They were not just for playing better golf. They were life principles, too. As I considered these questions and processed my feelings and thoughts, the answer became clear to me, but you will have to wait a little longer for me to tell you what I decided to do. We have more work to do. Tell me about this tee shot."

"Ok, it's a par-4 hole that is reachable in 2 shots. I usually hit a great shot with my driver, but I am not too sure because in the last tournament, I did not hit my driver well, and I feel like I have lost confidence in my driver," Meredith said, stringing together a long and winding run-on sentence.

"Woah, Woah, Woah!" Janell interrupted before any more negative thoughts could be said about the driver. "What did I tell you about punctuation, especially when it comes to your thoughts?"

"To put a PERIOD in the right place instead of a comma followed by negative thoughts," Meredith answered.

"That's right. So, let's try that again. What did you say at the very beginning of that very long sentence?" Janell asked with intention.

"I usually hit a great tee shot with my driver," Meredith answered beginning to believe again in her ability and in her forsaken club.

"PERIOD. Go trust your shot and do it!" Janell said confidently.

Meredith then approached the shot with a smile and a renewed sense of trust, went through her pre-shot routine, and hit an incredible shot in the middle of the fairway.

Janell threw up her hands in the air and said, "See, Meredith, golf's not that hard when you have talent like yours and you trust your shots!"

"That's easy for you to say!" Meredith responded with a smile. "You have a ton of talent and are a great golfer!"

"My talent is God-given, and my skills were developed through years of hard work and purposeful practice and repetition. In other words, stewarding the gifts and talents God has given me well. And God has given you gifts and talents too – as a golfer, a leader, and a person. You can maximize your potential and achieve your goals if you keep working and are *grateful for* and *faithful with* your gifts."

"Thanks, Coach JJ. I'm so glad I have you as my swing coach and role model," Meredith said.

Meredith, thinking back to the earlier part of their conversation asked, "Are you scared to die?"

"That's a thoughtful question," Janell answered. "I am not scared of dying, but I am scared of not living my life well and not following through on the things God has called me to do. And as my mentor would remind me, I should say that more positively: 'I am *focused* on living a purposeful and well-lived life for whatever time I have on earth.'"

"Well said. And me too," Meredith replied, and they both laughed as they walked to the next shot.

"So, did you play in the district tournament?" Meredith asked, still eager to know the answer.

"Let's find out," Janell replied as she continued her story.

CHAPTER 10

68

A score. A number. A metric. Wins and losses. Success. Failure.

In sports and in life, we are often judged by the result of our efforts. In fact, the bottom line is that the scoreboard reveals the result, but it never discloses the journey, which is as important as the goal. And our identity should never be tied to a number or performance!

Janell woke up thinking about the events of the last few days as well as all the moments that had led to today...the district tournament. She remembered what Mike said about making the most of your moments, honoring those who had invested in you, and answering the big question that confronts us when someone dies: What would they want you to do?

Janell came downstairs to see her mom making breakfast and wearing an expression on her face that revealed the key question of the day: Are you going to play?

Today was Janell's district tournament, and her family, friends, and coaches were awaiting her decision. Janell answered the unspoken question with resolve: "I am going to play!"

Janell did not know how she would play, but she was determined to not let anyone down, especially herself. This was the moment she had been preparing for all year. People expected her to win and to lead her team. And she was determined to play the game she loved.

Sometimes in life, you have to step out in faith not knowing what the day will reveal but determined to unleash your best and give it your all. As Jon Gordon says, "It's called a leap of faith, not a leap of fear."[1] Janell had developed resiliency, refined over the last two years. Her growth and resolute spirit would be on display for all to see today.

Janell's mom responded, "Sounds great and no matter what happens, I am proud of you!"

Janell's family had always been close and supportive of each other. They had faith and encouraged each other to give their all. Giving your best was not just a motto, it was a mission. And Janell so appreciated the support she had received, especially the last few days!

Janell gave her all on Day 1. She scored a 79. Not her best, not her worst. She made a valiant effort given the context and circumstances that led up to this day. But the district tournament doesn't care what you have been through. There is no room for excuses, just results.

Janell was glad she got through the day. While she was not pleased with her score, she was pleased with her effort physically, mentally, and emotionally. You cannot control outcomes, but you can focus on and influence the outcomes through your effort, attitude, mindset, and responses. Janell did that and was able to move through the "Day 1 moment."

She arrived home and began calculating what score she would need on day two to win the district tournament, the goal she had been pursuing all year. Had she done enough on the first day to put herself in position to win? What score would she have to shoot on day two to win the tournament? She also felt the weight and pressure of helping carry her team to victory.

High school golf is unique in that it combines both individual and team competition. You are playing for yourself, but also for your team. Janell was an incredible athlete who had played in other sports leading up to high school, but she ultimately chose golf as her sport because she liked that the outcome rested on her rather than on her teammates. Now, however, she found herself in a moment where the result of day two carried both individual and team weight like she had never experienced before. Her score the next day would determine whether both her individual and team goals would be achieved.

Later that night, Mike arrived to visit with Janell and her parents and check in on how the first day had gone. Janell was in her dad's study when Mike walked in with a smile on his face and exclaimed, "79! That's awesome! You totally have this!"

Janell looked at him with a puzzled expression. The two of them had never really celebrated a 79 with that much enthusiasm before. While the average golfer might hope and pray for a 79, Janell was capable of more, and they both knew it would take a better score to accomplish her goal of becoming District Champion.

Mike continued, "You totally have this! You got through today and put yourself in position for tomorrow. I am so proud of you – of your effort, your strength, your resilience, and your mental toughness!"

Janell responded, "It was tough, but I'm proud of the way I got through today. I just wish I had gone lower."

"Yes, a lower score would have been better, but you gave yourself an opportunity, and I know you're going to make the most of that opportunity tomorrow," Mike said.

"How do you know?" Janell asked.

"Because I know you, and I know the One you play for – the One who created you, who holds you, and who carries you through moments like these. God is going to give you a peace and strength tomorrow that you have never experienced before, and you are going to have your best day yet as a golfer," Mike said with a reassuring confidence.

The quest to be the best is not always an easy and straightforward path. It often involves twists, turns, side streets, detours, and complications. It can be a paradox filled with uncertainty and confidence. Doubt and trust. Anxiety and accomplishments. Fear and faith. And as most people understand: To be THE best, you have to focus on being YOUR best.

In fact, being YOUR best is all you can really ask of yourself. YOUR best is what frees you up to become THE best. When you focus on being your best in a moment, you release yourself from the chains of anxiety, expectations, and fear and adopt a posture of belief, trust, and faith. You overcome the weight of expectations of others by embracing the opportunity of the moment. You stop comparing and start competing. And you narrow your focus to the things you can control, such as your effort, attitude, and responses.

Janell recalled a mantra Mike had mentioned in one of their many coaching sessions together:

Focus on what you can control.

Influence what you can.

Flush the rest.

And this is exactly what she was going to do, putting into practice all that she had learned over the last 2 years. Resilience emerges when you say ENOUGH! Enough of the fear. Enough of the doubt. Enough of the anxiety that is holding you back. And enough of the distractions from the who that wants to steal your joy, kill your purpose, and destroy your impact.

Be your best. Trust your shot. Play moment by moment and shot to shot. Respond appropriately rather than react emotionally to unexpected moments. Janell felt all of these truths finally click for her and suddenly she had a clarity of mind and heart that she had never felt before. Yet, the question remained:

What score would she shoot, and would it be good enough?

They say character is revealed in the challenging moments of your life, and day two definitely represented a challenge for Janell. She had a lot of ground to make up in the standings, and she was still wrestling with her emotions from the events of the past few days. Somehow, Janell did not feel burdened. She felt enlightened. Instead of a challenge, she saw an opportunity – an opportunity to honor God in this moment and feel His presence more than she had ever experienced in her life. And to think that her new perspective began with a meeting that she didn't want to go to.

Janell was excited as she realized the power of the truths she had read so many times in the Bible. Passages like 2 Timothy 1:7 reminded her that God did not give her a spirit of fear but of power, love, and a sound mind. Foundational verses such as Isaiah 41:10 reassured her she did not need to be afraid because God was with her – strengthening her, helping her, and upholding her along the way. Finally, her favorite verse, Proverbs 4:26, which told her to "ponder the path" of her feet so that all of her ways would be sure.

She knew her steps would be sure today. She did not know how, but she just knew. She had full trust in God in this moment.

Janell drove up to the course, parked, and went through her normal routine. She began putting and then went to the practice range. She was quieter than normal, and she was focused and in a *zone* that few had ever seen in her. She did not say much, but her expression spoke volumes!

The first hole was a par 5, offering a good scoring opportunity. She began by hitting a great tee shot, which is always a nice way to start – whether you are playing on day two of the district tournament or simply playing a round of golf with your friends on the weekend. No one wants the embarrassment of hitting in the trees with everyone watching. Tee shots are the most visible so starting with a great one is always nice.

Janell's second shot was a solid approach that put her in position to get onto the green and shoot for a birdie. Her third shot placed her on the green, but she left herself a long putt. She closed out the hole with 2 putts. A 5 on the first hole and a par.

While she could have been frustrated that she did not capitalize on going under par on the first hole, she remembered something that Mike had said about tournament golf and her rounds, "Janell, you may have rounds where you have tap-in pars. The tendency is to be frustrated that you came so close and did not sink the previous putt for a birdie. Don't be frustrated by this. Focus on building momentum from these moments trusting that eventually the putts will fall and being grateful that you don't have to sink hard pars."

Enjoy the easy pars, and eventually the birdies will happen became her motto for the day. She picked up her golf ball, marked her score on this hole, and walked to the second tee.

What followed was a master class in how to focus your mind and heart and be fully present in the moment. The distractions of the course and the disappointments of the past few days dissipated. She steadied her mind and her clubs on the task at hand, and she brought her full self to every shot. And the results revealed her focus. Par. Par. Par. Par. Birdie! Par. Par. Par. A score of 35 on the front nine on day two of the district tournament.

The score only told one dimension of her story. While the spectators saw greatness, others also saw grit, determination, and perseverance. Her family, close friends, and Mike knew the backstory and what she had experienced leading up to this moment, and they were amazed by her focus. If the back nine holes were as good as her first nine holes, she would be in perfect position to win the day and win the tournament.

Janell grabbed a quick sandwich as she transitioned to the final nine. She also gave a head nod and a slight smile to her family and Mike as if acknowledging their presence and affirming her presence as well. She was back...physically, mentally, emotionally, and spiritually!

She shot pars on the next two holes. On the 12th hole, she shot a birdie. She shot pars on the 13th and 14th holes and then another birdie on the 15th. On the 16th hole, she shot a bogey, which was her first one of the day. When that happens to a golfer, the round can sometimes take a turn for the worst. But Janell had worked on building a mindset of resiliency and responding in the moment for the last 2 years allowing her to answer on 17 with another birdie.

As she approached the 18th hole, the obvious tension and excitement of the moment built. A large crowd, including her coach, teammates, and competitors, began gathering around the hole to witness this epic moment. Although not The Masters, it was an important moment to all who were involved, especially Janell!

Finish! The word that reverberated through every part of her being! "Trust your shot!" echoed through her mind. The goal was clear: finish this hole with a par or better, and she would win the day. This was her opportunity to conquer the moment – or rather, define the moment instead of letting it define her.

She selected her driver – a club that had not let her down and one she could depend on in moments like this. She had the most beautiful swing, and her shots seemed especially effortless today. She had invested a lot of time and energy in perfecting HER swing rather than searching for the perfect swing.

She confidently placed her golf ball on the tee and went through her pre-shot routine. She swung the club like she had done so many times in practice, trusting the ball would go where she pictured it. The shot sounded like a rocket taking off as it zoomed down the middle of the fairway, just as she had envisioned it. Picture it…Paint it! That's what she and Mike had worked on in so many on-course mental game sessions, and this was the moment to put the finishing touches on her work of art today. Or better said, the masterpiece that God was working in and through her.

Janell had learned to not expend energy in between her shots. In one of the very first sessions that she had with Mike, he had her pull out her phone and do some math using the calculator on her phone.

"Janell, how long does it take to play a typical 18 holes of golf in a high school tournament?" Mike asked.

"About four and a half to five hours. Sometimes longer," Janell replied, suspecting that Mike either already knew the answer to his question or knew nothing about golf. She was still trying to figure him out, since it was their first session together.

"Janell, would you agree that a golf shot takes about 12 seconds to hit once you have pictured your shot and selected the club you want to use?" Mike asked.

"Yes," Janell replied, wondering where this series of questions was going.

"I want you to multiply 71 x 12. What number do you get?"

"852," Janell replied not understanding what this number meant.

"Ok, divide that number by 60, and tell me the number that it calculates," Mike said with a slight smile on his face.

"14.2," Janell answered.

"14.2," Mike echoed her answer. "Do you know what that number means? It is the number of minutes you need to focus during a typical 18-hole round. We took the number of shots to achieve par in a round and multiplied it by 12 seconds to focus on and execute your shot and then divided the product by 60 to calculate the number of minutes."

And managing her emotional and mental energy effectively was exactly what Janell had done today in the district tournament. She demonstrated focus in the moments that mattered, and she relaxed and recharged in the moments in between. Although the last few days had been exhausting physically, mentally, and emotionally, Janell knew how to focus when it mattered most.

So often, athletes and leaders assume they need to stay stressed for hours in order to succeed. They act as if joy has no place in competition and that smiling and enjoying the moment will somehow make them less serious or effective. Yet peak performers know how to direct their energy and mental focus toward what matters most while tuning out distractions that threaten to pull them off the path to success, impact, and meaning.

As she walked up to her second shot, Janell could sense the end. It was almost as if she could envision it. She simply needed to do her part and trust that the rest would follow. She glanced toward her family, who were there cheering her on and providing support that extended far beyond the golf course. Then, she looked at Mike, who had been there through so many moments and had taught her the value of cherishing and making the most of every moment, both on and off the course.

Her eyes and mind then shifted to her approach shot. Picture it. Paint it. She went through her normal pre-shot routine, stepped up to the ball, and whispered "Trust Your Shot" to herself. Then, she hit an incredible shot that landed about 10 feet from the hole.

The crowd cheered and knew the opportunity before her. Janell had two putts to get a par and secure the District Championship. As she approached the green, she looked around and saw so many familiar faces – teammates, friends, her coaches, and her competitors. She loved golf because the result was all on her, and she was determined to finish the job.

She stepped up to the first putt and hit a shot that went in and around the cup leaving her a tap-in par. She sank her last putt, finished the final hole with a par, and won the District Championship. Her teammates and coaches ran up, surrounding and smothering her with hugs and encouragement. She soaked in this moment and then hugged her mom like she had never hugged her before with tears of joy flowing. So much had been bottled up, but today she let it out, unleashing her best and glorifying God in the process.

She hugged her dad and the rest of her family as well as Mike who, for the last two years, had been teaching her mental game techniques to prepare her for moments like this. She appreciated that without his presence in her life, especially over the last couple of days, she may never have experienced a moment like this on the course.

Janell now realized how ***the process*** had prepared her for this moment and how the 5 keys to a championship mindset had given her the principles she needed to nurture a powerful and resilient mindset.

She soon discovered that her solo victory helped secure a team championship for her school and that her score of 68 was the new course record for a District Championship.

The next day, the headline of the sports page of the Katy Times appropriately read:

"Lysack Lights The Way!"

Sports reporter Terry Carter, who had covered Janell's career, wrote:

"On Wednesday no one displayed their mettle better than Seven Lakes senior Janell Lysack on the demanding River Ridge Golf Club near Sealy, TX. Lysack, who is headed to Texas A&M in the fall to play golf, hit 13-of-15 fairways and fired a 3-under-par 68 to run off with the girls' low medalist honors by eight strokes. The Spartan senior birdied three holes on the back nine with precision drives and sharp putting, and her 68 ranked as a personal best and the low round of the boys' or girls' district tournament. In fact, her 36-hole score of 147 also achieved those marks.

"This is a very challenging district. We are very competitive," Lysack said of her district competition. "Yesterday was pretty rough. Going into today, my mindset was very positive. I didn't set any standards or expectations today, but today was the day! Everything worked!"

68. It's just a number – the number of a record that was broken a few years later. But for this time and this moment, it signified so much more than a signed scorecard ever could.

CHAPTER 11

Day 2

"Keep your soul diligently, so that you do not forget the things which your eyes have seen and they do not depart from your heart all the days of your life;"

DEUTERONOMY 4:9, NEW AMERICAN STANDARD BIBLE 1995

How long does a moment actually last? You never know how much a moment can matter in your life and in the lives of other people. Your choices, attitude, and response in a split-second moment significantly impact future moments.

In golf, a moment could be a putt to finish an incredible round of golf. It could be a shot you wish you had back or a round that you wish you could forget. It could be a tournament where you gave your all and did your best. A moment could be your senior season, your high school career, or your entire life.

Janell reflected on all of the moments from her very first meeting with Mike to what she had accomplished at the district tournament. She was so grateful to play a part in an awesome moment that glorified God. Her attention now turned to the upcoming regional tournament at a familiar course.

Janell's main competitor would be someone she had played against for the last several years and who was also highly ranked. In fact, they were the top two golfers in both the area as well as the state of Texas. They were fierce competitors and also good friends. Janell knew the regional tournament was an opportunity. The biggest lesson that Janell had learned, especially over the last 2 years, was to enjoy the moment and to view tournaments and competition as an opportunity rather than an obstacle. Now she was ready to unleash her potential.

The regional tournament consists of 2 days of 18-hole rounds. Janell played consistent on day one shooting a 79 – not her best score. After the first day, she was still in contention both to win the tournament and to help lead her team to a championship. A team win would allow the whole team to go to the state tournament for the first time ever.

"How do you feel?" Mike asked as they debriefed the first day.

"I feel good. I got a feel for the course. I got the bad shots out of my system, and I am ready to go low tomorrow," Janell responded.

"That's great. What did you do well, and what did you learn?" Mike asked.

"I hit my driver well, and for most of the round, I was consistent in my pre-shot routine. I played shot to shot and did a good job of visualizing and picturing my shots. What I learned is that when I play with joy and focus, I play my best golf. Tomorrow is my last opportunity to play in a high school regional tournament. I want to make it count and play every shot with joy and focus. As you have taught me to say, 'I want to make the most of my moments.'"

"That is very insightful. There is nothing stopping you from doing that tomorrow. Have fun. Enjoy the moment. And play with a determination to make the most of this moment, glorifying God in the process," Mike encouraged.

Day two always requires intense focus and includes important moments. This doesn't mean the first day does not count. It does! But things tend to become even more important on the second day of a tournament because it's your final chance to make your mark, to play your best, and to leave a legacy.

Mike arrived at the golf course about an hour before day two of the regional tournament and parked his car. He typed a final text to Janell reminding her of the same key success factors that he always sent to her before every tournament:

- Be Present in the Moment.
- Play Shot to Shot.
- SFT: See it, Feel it, Trust it. [1]
- Make the Most of this Moment!

These simple phrases had transformational depth and profound meaning. They weren't just trite sayings or cute cliches. Over time and through many moments of practice and hard work, Janell and Mike had discussed and applied principles that were summarized by these words.

On game day, you must simplify. As a competitor and leader, you can't try to think about all of the detailed steps that will allow you to have success. By this point, it's too late. The key to performing at your best is ensuring these steps are automatic and ingrained, and that the mention of a phrase unleashes your best. Peak performers simplify and trust to unleash their best.

Mike hit send on the text message and got out of the car to walk around. He saw Janell getting ready to go through her preparation and practice on the putting green, and he walked over to her.

"This is your moment! You're ready. Let's go! Most of all, play with JOY and focus in every moment," Mike said with conviction.

"You're right. I am ready. Thanks for all you have done for me," Janell replied.

Janell walked onto the practice green as Mike walked away to let her be in the moment and go through her final preparation and warm-up.

Mike loved to observe the course – the arena where competitors performed – and observe how different golfers prepared for these moments. He would watch warm-up routines of individuals, interactions between family and friends and the athlete they had come to cheer for, and the expressions and styles of different coaches. It is often in these moments that a tournament, competition, or game is won or lost because of the right word of encouragement or advice.

As Mike made his way toward the first tee, he observed a coach talking to one of his golfers in a frustrated manner. He wasn't yelling at her, but he obviously wasn't happy about something that seemed to revolve around how she was putting. At one point, the coach grabbed the putter from his nervous golfer's hands and began to try and demonstrate or, better said, dictate how she should putt.

Mike reflected on how this moment would affect the golfer and what she would be thinking about for the next few hours over 18 holes of golf. He also thought about how a couple of minutes before tee time on day two of the regional tournament is a little late to be working on a technical lapse in her putting game. At this point, the coach could have made a much greater impact if he had just given her a fist bump, smiled, and told her to go have fun and play her best today.

The tone, timing, and temperament of your words are vital to the success and wellbeing of the people you coach, encourage, lead, and impact. Your words influence whether a person goes out and gives their best or shrinks back in fear and doubt. The right words in the moment can lift a person's spirit and help them nurture the right mindset to take the field, course, court, or office with confidence.

As a mental performance coach, Mike always carefully considered his words to help his athletes prepare to perform. He also sometimes wondered if he had said enough or too much. The proof would be in their performance and their application of not only what was said in those last moments before they stepped up to the tee but also all of the work they had put in leading to this moment in the spotlight. Mike knew that Janell had heard, received, incorporated, and applied all of what they had discussed and practiced. He knew she was ready.

Mike stepped up to the cart path by the first tee and saw Janell's parents.

"Hi Donna. Hi Chuck. How are ya'll doing?" Mike asked.

"We are doing well," Donna responded.

"Hi Mike," Chuck added.

"How do you think she is doing?" Donna asked.

"I think she is ready and is going to have a great day!" Mike said.

"I do too," Donna said. "She told me this morning that she just wants to go out and have fun. When Janell plays with focus and enjoys the moments, she plays incredible golf! She has learned how to play with joy and focus from you, and we appreciate all that you have done for her and taught her."

"Janell is an incredible person, student, and golfer, and it has been my pleasure to work with her," Mike replied.

"Here she comes," Donna said with excited anticipation.

Janell walked down the cart path toward the first tee carrying her bag. As she approached, she glanced over at her mom, dad, and Mike then gave a tip of her cap to acknowledge them and smiled – her way of saying thanks for being here and I am ready...all in the same moment.

Janell set her clubs down and adjusted her ponytail and hat. Mike had noticed through hours of watching Janell play tournament golf that Janell would adjust her ponytail before big moments. He had remembered how they had often talked about the importance of physical cues to remember mental keys. The adjustment of her ponytail was a physical cue for her to *set* her mind to play her best. It was her key to lock in.

When it was time to tee off, Janell pulled out her driver, went through her per-shot routine visualizing the shot she wanted to hit, and smacked a beautiful drive down the middle of the fairway. She looked over at her parents and Mike again and smiled. This would be the last time she did this until the round was over, but she was confirming with them that this could be a special day.

Janell was paired with several golfers she had known and competed against for years. One of them was among the top players in the state. In fact, Janell and this golfer had been the top two players in both their region and the state, and everyone wanted to witness this incredible showdown. Because of the significance of the matchup, a large crowd followed this group, including family, friends, coaches, several local sportswriters, and a few college coaches.

As they played their first few holes, everyone watching noticed something unexpected about Janell and her top competitor: they were talking in what appeared to be a genuinely friendly way. It was not the kind of interaction you would expect from two athletes trying to beat each other, lead their team to a regional tournament championship, and earn a berth to the state tournament in Austin.

Beyond the friendly banter, they were laughing and having fun between some shots. Some of the people who were watching began to wonder, *"How could someone competing in a moment like this smile and laugh? They must not be very focused."*

Over the years, in many coaching sessions, Mike had talked with Janell about the in-between moments during a 4-5 hour round of golf. He told her these were some of the most important moments in a round of golf and encouraged her to find an authentic way to release any stress or frustration and simply enjoy the journey. He suggested she might talk with other golfers, take some deep breaths, and enjoy the walk, the trees, and the beauty of the course.

Janell filled the in-between moments with smiling, talking, and enjoying the scenery. She had learned to appreciate and be grateful for the opportunity to do what she was getting to do and where she was getting to do it. Golf had provided her many moments to experience new places as well as beautiful courses to demonstrate her God-given talent. She had mastered the in-between moments, which helped her perform at her best when it mattered most.

As the group progressed through the holes, Janell was playing really well. She was hitting her drives in the fairway and setting herself up for the right approach shots. She was taking advantage of using the right club to put herself in scoring position on the green. And then she was finishing the hole by draining her putts. This sequence continued hole after hole.

Along the way, she was not only smiling and but even laughing at times. She was enjoying the scenery of the tall trees, green fairways, and small fountains in the streams between the holes. She observed the houses that were built beside the course. And she even noticed a couple of hawks with outstretched wings soaring effortlessly through the sky almost as if to show off their God-given gifts and abilities. In essence, Janell was soaking it all in and playing with joy.

And when it was time to focus, she was locked in. She would observe the layout of the course and shot before taking notice of the obstacles and opportunities before her. And while she noticed the trees in certain spots and the sand and water that were beckoning for her attention, she did not let their siren call distract her from focusing on the target. She pictured her shots with a specificity of an artist and painted them with creativity and excellence.

By the time she had finished the first nine holes and was making the turn to play the last nine, she found herself playing even par golf. She knew she was playing well, but she didn't allow the score to dictate her focus or distract her from playing and performing at her best in the moment. So many times, golfers, athletes, and generally everyone can either linger in the past dwelling on what could have been or jump forward to the future and what could be instead of focusing on the moment that is right in front of them and making the most of the opportunity. Janell was choosing to be in the moment, yet again, and it was paying off for both her and her team.

As she approached the final holes, her coach told her that they were close to getting a team win based on her score and what some of her teammates were doing on other holes. And while she took note of this, she had learned through her coaching sessions with Mike to focus on what was right in front of her. In fact, Mike had given her an axiom that had always been helpful, especially in moments like these:

Play your round, and let the round play out.

She had learned that she could only control herself and what was in front of her and not what her teammates or competitors were doing on other holes. She was in charge of her attitude, her energy, her effort, her mindset, and her self-talk. And she could focus on dialing in her pre-shot routine with precision to impact her final score. So that was exactly what she was doing.

As she played the final holes of 16, 17, and 18, she continued to execute her shots like an archer with incredible aim. And every time she stepped onto the green, she sank her putts. And when she turned in her scorecard, she had shot the low score for day two: 72, even par. Combined with her score on day one, she earned a second place finish, which assured her another trip to the state tournament as an individual player, but she was hoping for more for her team.

She connected with her family and Mike, and they congratulated her on what she had just accomplished. Their collective attention then turned to the final finishers on her team. As each golfer approached, Janell encouraged them with a smile, which was all they needed to play loose, fierce, and free. At the end of the day, her team won the regional tournament championship, something her school had never done.

Janell was there to provide high fives and hugs. She knew this moment was not about her but rather something bigger. And that's the kind of leader she was. A champion who knew how to perform at her best and to inspire others to do the same. A servant leader who doesn't make the moment all about herself but recognizes and celebrates the presence and contributions of her teammates.

Janell reflected on the last two years. An incredible run to the state tournament as a sophomore. Her missed putt that led to a meeting that she did not want to attend. And all the moments of growth, setbacks, and success along the way which had contributed to her becoming the person and leader God had created her to be.

Oh, and another trip to the state tournament, which was nice! A place she wondered if she would ever get back to but had dreamed for with a determined spirit and a Biblical hope. And this dream was now coming true.

In the end, it didn't matter how Janell and the team would finish at the state tournament. This journey was never about the number of trophies but rather the art of becoming. And while Janell did earn a lot of trophies and accolades, she realized that becoming the person she was created to be was the most important thing.

In fact, it's the most important thing for all of us. We can focus so much on what we want to achieve that we lose sight of who we are becoming in the process. Have you ever taken time to consider these essential life questions:

- Who am I?
- Who have I been created to be?
- Who do I need to become?

Identifying answers to these questions helps us become who we were meant to be. Growth happens when we become aware of the gap between where we are and where we need to be. Self-reflection helps us to realize our gaps and opportunities as well as our strengths and accomplishments. If we only focus on our limitations and what we have not done, we will lament the past and be afraid to take the next step forward. If we narrowly dwell on our strengths and past accomplishments, we will become complacent about both learning and making a positive difference within our sphere of influence.

In all circumstances, we need to keep taking steps forward and focusing our mind, heart, and soul on discovering our purpose. Perseverance happens when we push through the past and press on to what's ahead.

Jerry Sittser offers this perspective in his great book *A Grace Disguised: How The Soul Grows Through Loss*. Jerry lost his wife, daughter, and mother in a tragic car accident that he and his other children survived and wrote this book based on what God taught him through the process. As he moved through the process of grief, he realized:

*"The experience of loss does not have to be the defining moment in our lives. Instead, the defining moment can be our response to the loss. It is not what happens to us that matters so much as **what happens in us.**"*[2]

The key question is not "What Am I Achieving?" but "Who Am I Becoming?" In other words, consider these questions:

- What is happening in me?
- Am I becoming the person I was created to be?
- Am I running the race that was intended for me to run?
- Am I staying on course and on point?
- Am I becoming the man, woman, husband, wife, father, mother, leader, teammate, athlete, coach, and friend that those closest to me need me to be?
- And am I leading with purpose and passion and playing the role that was created for me?

Becoming is a journey, not a destination, and it is the most important trip you will ever take.

Becoming was the most important lesson that Janell learned throughout her journey.

CHAPTER 12

Moments That Matter

Moments.
Choices.
Decisions.
Thoughts.
Habits.
Relationships.
Attitude.
Effort.
Mindset.
Identity.
Focus.
Process.
Determination.
Resiliency.
Purpose.

These were key concepts that Janell had leveraged to maximize her potential, accomplish her goals, and become the person she was created to be. Some of her many "on the course" accomplishments included:

- Was a 4-year varsity golfer at Seven Lakes High School.
- Voted the district MVP all four years of her high school career.
- Voted First Team All-District all four years and First Team All-State her sophomore year.
- Achieved Academic All-District all 4 years.
- Selected All-region and All-Greater Houston her junior and senior year.
- Finished in the Top-10 at districts and regionals in each of her 4 years.
- Competed on the Texas Junior Golf Tour for four years.
- Was a 4-year golfer at Texas A&M University.

Her "off the course" accomplishments are too hard to measure and too numerous to count. How do you measure the true impact of an encouraging word, a performance that inspires, and a life lived well? I love what C. William Pollard, former Chairman of ServiceMaster, said about servant leadership[1]:

> *"A servant leader's results are measured beyond the workplace, and the story is told in the changed lives of others."*

True servant leaders make a positive and lasting impact not simply by what they accomplish but rather by truly serving the people they lead, influence, and meet through their platform or "sphere of influence." Robert Browning talked about how a person's reach should exceed his or her grasp. The generational effects of Janell's leadership are timeless and eternal, far exceeding her immediate reach and sphere of influence.

Her high school career was over, but never forgotten, and she had decided to play golf at Texas A&M University. Janell was looking forward to the next stage of her life and was eager to see how the journey would unfold. Her first tournament as a Texas A&M Aggie would reveal much about her leadership, her impact, and her legacy.

The "Mo" Morial Invitational is a tournament that honors Monica Welsh, a great Aggie golfer who earned team MVP honors during an incredible collegiate career and who died tragically in a car accident. The significance of this tournament and the impact of this Texas A&M golfer was not lost on Janell even though she was a freshman and just beginning her collegiate journey. She also knew that some of the top teams in the nation were coming to College Station, TX, to play in this tournament. Janell wondered, "What would make this moment even more special?"

Just a few days before the tournament, Janell spoke to one of her friends who was an Aggie Yell Leader. The Yell Leaders are elected by the entire student population and serve as the leaders of yells (not cheers) at university events. They are best known for leading the Texas A&M community (both current and former students) in co-ordinated yells during football games, but they attend other major sporting events as well. Yet, Aggie Yell Leaders had never led yells at golf tournaments.

Janell asked her friend if he and his fellow Yell Leaders could come to the "Mo" Memorial tournament. She explained what it was, the significance of honoring a fallen Aggie, and the opportunity to represent the University in front of many other schools that would be competing in this invitational match. He told her he would ask. Three days later, the Aggie Yell Leaders were in attendance, maybe for the first time, at a women's golf tournament. And they didn't just attend, they led yells.

This was Janell. A leader who would ask "What if?" and "Why Not?" to improve the experiences and possibilities for herself and others. In fact, an incredible moment would happen, and people often commented, "Only Janell could make this happen!"

Janell would go on to play four years for the Texas A&M Women's Golf Team, serve on the SEC Women's Golf Community Service Team, and help coordinate Aggies CAN, one of the largest student-athlete run canned food drives in the nation. Aggies CAN is a massive annual service initiative that collects food and helps fight hunger, benefiting the Brazos Valley Food Bank and the 12th CAN.

In her junior year at Texas A&M, Janell was elected as President of the Student-Athlete Advisory Committee (SAAC), and she served so well that she was re-elected for her senior year. Rarely did a student athlete serve as SAAC president for two years, especially one who did not play one of the university's major sports.

Excellence, leadership, service, humility – these qualities defined Janell in every area of her life. She embodied the spirit of Colossians 3:17 which says:

"And whatever you do, whether in word or deed, do it all in the name of the Lord Jesus, giving thanks to God the Father through Him."

After finishing her playing career, Janell earned her master's degree while working at Hermitage Golf Course in Nashville as an Assistant Head Pro. She also served as an assistant coach for the Trevecca Nazarene University women's golf team and earned her PGA teaching certification.

While at Hermitage, Janell created what came to be known as JJ's Juniors, a program that gave aspiring golfers the opportunity both to learn and grow in the game of golf. She worked with them individually and in groups, helping them improve both technically and mentally. She also partnered with Hermitage to conduct tournaments that allowed them to grow through competition. Many of these juniors began in elementary school and went on to become high school and college golfers.

Mike Eller, Owner of Hermitage Golf Course and former president of the Tennessee PGA Chapter, recalled his first meeting with Janell. He said, "I typically hire golf assistants usually based on recommendations from people I trust. Janell's name came up six times. I immediately called to set up an interview with her. Once she sat down in my office, we exchanged niceties, and it was 'over' for me. Janell took over and was interviewing me instead. Never in my life had I met a more determined, goal-oriented person in my 40 years as a PGA member. She knew what she wanted and if she couldn't get that opportunity at Hermitage, she would get it someplace else. I could not say 'You are hired!' fast enough. As the saying goes, 'You had me at hello.' I can honestly say we fell in love with Janell, and she was immediately part of the family."

After approximately four years in Nashville at Hermitage, Janell landed another exciting opportunity working for Callaway Golf. She rose through the ranks and was selected for Callaway's Emerging Leaders Program, an elite group of 17 employees recognized as high potential leaders in the company. As a part of this program, Janell experienced additional training and developmental opportunities to help her grow as a leader.

Brad Barnett, Vice President of Operations at Callaway Golf, fondly remembered his experiences with Janell at Callaway. He described her as someone who was "born and made" for high impact moments, one of which included opening a new facility while navigating the complexities of a new building, new system, new automation, multiple brands, and a historic spike in demand for golf products. Brad said, "While Janell did not have a frontline operating role when she began working there, she volunteered to step in and help at a moment when we desperately needed more 'smart' system-literate, solution-oriented people. Janell was willing to do whatever it took to succeed. It was the longest, highest intensity period in my career in operations and supply chain work, and I am so glad Janell was a key member of this team!"

Janell's parents, Donna and Chuck Lysack, said this about Janell: *"Janell lived life to the fullest and had accomplished more both personally and professionally than most in just 29 years. She made people feel seen and heard. Janell was intentional in all of her relationships. She followed Christ in her daily life and lived wholeheartedly by her favorite Bible verse Proverbs 4:26 (ESV): 'Ponder the path of your feet; then all your ways will be sure.'"*

The moments captured in this book are just a few examples of how well Janell lived her life with grit and grace. We can all learn from the journey of Janell!

The Final Chapter

"Emperor Meiji: Tell me how he died.
Captain Algren: I will tell you how he lived."

THE LAST SAMURAI MOVIE

The people were beginning to file into the sanctuary to be seated. The gathering was a beautiful site. So many people had come to honor a life well lived. Though the moment brought sadness and left people wondering why an unimaginable accident took the life of someone so young, it also reminded everyone what a life of significance truly looks like.

Mike was seated in the third row and slowly returned to the present moment. He had been reflecting on the many moments that shaped Janell's life. From the meeting that almost wasn't to moments that could only come from God. It was almost as if he had relived Janell's entire story in his mind as he prepared to speak at her celebration of life ceremony.

As the piano and organ began to play, the large crowd grew quiet, the mood in the sanctuary turning reflective. The pastor welcomed everyone, offered a few introductory words about Janell and this occasion, and then introduced Mike.

Mike walked to the microphone and looked out at the crowd. It was a mixture of people who had played with Janell, competed against her, cheered for her, mentored her, and had been touched by her life. Wasn't that what a celebration of someone's life was all about? It was a gathering of people coming together to communicate joy and appreciation for a life well lived!

"There may be a few tears today, but that's okay. There may be a few smiles and laughter today, and that's fine too," Mike began. "Janell Marie Lysack Joslin personified greatness! She was selfless and exceptional! She was fierce and compassionate in competition. She was a leader on and off the course, and she always pursued her best to inspire others to do their best. Janell was an excellent encourager with both her words and her actions.

"Janell was the best athlete I ever coached as a mental performance coach," Mike continued. "Janell is gone, but never forgotten. Janell was a very special person who served as a light to everyone she met.

"I was fortunate enough to work with Janell for six years through her high school and collegiate golf career," Mike continued holding back some tears. "She was competitive and compassionate. She balanced grit, grace, truth, and love in all of her relationships. She was focused on doing her best while leading and helping others to be and do their best. Everyone she competed against loved and appreciated her, which is rare in the world of sports. She truly lived out Proverbs 4:26 (ESV), which was her theme verse:

> *'Ponder the path of your feet;*
> *then all your ways will be sure.'*

"I know she is in Heaven shining a light on Jesus, the true Light of her life!"

Mike spoke about her many accomplishments, but he also reflected on who she became during the six years they worked together and as he watched her transition after her college career. And while her achievements were remarkable, her impact on those she encountered was even greater. He also shared the story of how Janell had been reluctant to meet with him at first, only to discover something we all must learn: we all need people in our lives to encourage, edify, and help us move through difficult moments so that we can emerge stronger on the other side.

"We talked a lot about moments, identity, and where identity comes from – about how it is not tied to a score or a golf shot. We discussed how to be an artist on the golf course and how 'painting' your shots allows your skill and talent to shine through. We also talked about mental game strategies that could improve your recovery time when things did not go as expected or when you faced unanticipated challenges and circumstances. We live in a broken and imperfect world, and things do not always work out the way we want them to. Both valley and mountaintop moments will occur in life. We cannot always predict when they will happen, but we can prepare for them. And I wanted her to be prepared so that she could perform at her best and recover quickly when trouble raised its ugly head.

"We also talked about the five forces – fear, pressure, doubt, lack of confidence, and negative thoughts – and how she could overcome them by replacing them with faith, trust, and belief both on the course and off. One of the last things that I told her in our first coaching session was: 'Janell, it's a process,' a phrase that would become a continual reminder of the growth journey she was already on when I met her."

Mike paused to let that settle in before adding, "It's also a powerful reminder for all of us as we grieve and cherish her memory."

"I want to close my part of this moment, as we celebrate Janell's life and journey, with one final story. Every time we had an on-course coaching session, we worked on applying the mental game strategies she was learning. It was an opportunity in the heat of competition to put into practice the conversations and principles we had discussed. Before every shot, we walked through the same process to help dial in her approach and refine her pre-shot routine. The dialogue went something like this:

Me: "Janell, what do you see?"

Janell: "I see trees on the right, sand on the left, and water on the back side of the green."

Me: "Now, picture your shot. What do you see?"

Janell: "I see a right to left shot landing on the green and bouncing a few feet from the hole."

Me: "Sounds great! Paint and trust your shot!"

"If I asked that same question of her right now, 'Janell, what do you see?,' I am pretty sure she would say:

"I see God in all of His glory. No distractions, no disappointments, no suffering, and no sadness. I see Jesus welcoming me home with open arms!"

"To which I would reply, 'Sounds awesome! Enjoy the moment, and I can't wait to join you!'"

Mike stepped off the stage and turned toward Janell's parents, who acknowledged the moment with tears of both sorrow and joy. Their expressions spoke volumes.

Jeff, a pastor who had known Janell for most of her life, concluded Janell's Celebration of Life ceremony by sharing stories about his relationship with her as well as what her many friends had said about her based upon his interviews and conversations with them. He also shared the Gospel – how Janell had accepted Jesus into her life and the eternal implications of that decision. He did an excellent job of extending the same invitation to those in attendance. He affirmed that knowing where you are going after you die can provide solace and comfort even in moments like these.

The service concluded, and Donna and Chuck walked over to Mike.

"That was awesome and such a special tribute to Janell!" Donna said. "We appreciate everything you did for her!"

"Yes, we are grateful for you!" Chuck echoed.

"Janell was a special person, a great golfer, and an incredible leader! All I did was listen, ask the right questions, and share principles and insights along the way to help her unlock and unleash what was already inside her."

"Yes, she was special. But you did far more for her than we could have ever expected or hoped for. You were with her every step of her journey – through the mountaintop moments and even a few valley moments. Do you remember this?" Donna asked as she handed Mike a piece of paper on which was a quote Janell had written about Mike as she was headed off to college:

"I would not have accomplished what I have accomplished, been where I have been, or experienced what I have experienced without the impact of Mike in my life. Since meeting with Mike, a whole new outlook on and off the golf course has appeared for me. He has introduced over a dozen techniques to help with positive thoughts during my golf round. Mike has taught me exercises to train my mind to replace the negative side of the situations and see the most positive side of the situation.

It can seem as if I am in the worst possible situation to an outsider but in my eyes, I see it as just another challenge put in front of me to test my ability. I see obstacles as just another opportunity. I see pressure as just another chance to perform."

"Yes, I remember that, and I am so grateful for her words about our coaching journey together. Once again, this reflects Janell's generosity and graciousness," Mike said, his voice filled with appreciation as a tear rolled down his cheek.

Mike hugged Donna and Chuck and left the sanctuary, knowing this would not be the end of their relationship.

Approximately 700 people filed out of the church and could be heard reflecting on the moment and all they had shared with Janell. Janell's life inspired many who were there to examine their own lives. Were they living with purpose? Were they making the most of their moments? How would Janell want them to honor her through their lives? And had they made the same decision Janell had made about putting her faith in Jesus?

Though Janell is gone, she will never be forgotten, and her legacy will continue to live on through all of us.

And reflecting on that insightful and piercing question asked by one of JJ's Juniors:

"How did you know when you were great?"

How do we know when any of us are a great player, a great leader, a great wife or husband, a great mom or dad, a great teacher or coach, or a great person?

The answer is found in the changed lives of others and told through the transformational and eternal impact we have had on their lives. That is when we know someone was great, or better said, someone who was grateful for and faithful with the time they had on this earth, intent on making the most of their moments while glorifying God in the process.

> *"What is ultimately important is not how long we live, but how well we live. When you think you have years, you tend to waste days. It's time to start making your days count. Jesus didn't save us so we could live a boring, mediocre, barely-get-by life. Live every day with purpose."[2]*
>
> *- Christine Caine*

JJ's Impact

Janell had a tremendous impact on thousands of people throughout her lifetime. As her mom, Donna, said, "she seemed to be everyone's best friend," or at least that was how the people in her life felt. Janell made everyone she encountered feel seen, heard, understood, and appreciated. And isn't that what we all desire – to be truly known?

While it is impossible to recount every conversation and every moment of impact that Janell had on others, I wanted to share the names of four people that were part of JJ's Juniors at Hermitage Golf Course in Nashville, Tennessee, where Janell (Coach JJ) served as an assistant pro, golf instructor, and mental performance coach.

They represent just a few of the many people Janell impacted throughout her life, and I believed they would provide some of the clearest examples of how she passed on the lessons and wisdom she had learned to the next generation of golfers and leaders. Each of these students shared many stories with me about Coach JJ and her impact on them, which began when they were in elementary school and continued into junior high. They all confirmed that they would not have been able to accomplish all they have, both on and off the golf course, without Coach JJ in their lives.

Reagan Robinson

High School: Reagan served as captain of the golf team, finished as the state runner-up, and earned all-state and all-region honors. She was also selected as a Tennessee Golfer of the Year nominee, recorded the lowest state tournament score in school history, and ranked No. 3 in her graduating class. Her many honors included: Member of the Cum Laude Society, Mu Alpha Theta Honors Society, National Honors Society, Spanish Honors Society, St. Vincent de Paul Service Honors Society, and Cardinal Newman Honors Society. She was the recipient of the LGPA Marilynn Smith Scholarship and earned honorable mention for the USGA-AJGA Presidents' Leadership Award. She also earned First Tee ACE Certification, the highest level of certification for participants in the First Tee program and a designation earned by less than one percent of First Tee participants nationwide.

College: In her first season as a collegiate golfer at Washington University in St. Louis, she was named WGCA All-American Scholar. She contributed to her team's 2024 Golfweek Championship win and a top five finish at the 2025 DIII National Championship. In addition to her many accomplishments on the course, she made the Dean's List, served as Co-President of the Student Athletic Advisory Committee, and became a certified group fitness instructor. She served as a chemistry peer-led learning leader and participated on the WashU Investment Fund Pitch Team. She also worked as Financial Accounting Teaching Assistant.

My Quote About Janell: "JJ had this incredible way of making you feel confident no matter what. Her leadership, confidence, and belief in others is something I will carry with me forever. I truly hope that every young athlete is blessed with a coach and mentor like JJ in their life. She wasn't just my golf coach. She positively influenced the way I saw myself, and I am forever grateful."

Meredith Eller

High School: 3 TSSAA State appearances with two top-10 finishes...2nd place finish at PKB Triad Girls Classic...Top 5 finish at Tennessee State Girls Junior Championship...1 SNEDS Tour win, 3 top five finishes and 3 top 10 finishes (Aug 2024 - July 2025)...Two-time District Champion...Two-time Regional Champion...Three-time Wilson County Cup Champion...All-District team, all four years...MVP, all four years...Captain 4 years... Athlete of the Month September (all four years)... High School Low Record Holder – 69... High School Highest State Finish – 7th... Ranked 12th in the State for JGS and ranked 7th in the State for my class for JGS in 2026... Outstanding Achievement awards in AP Human Geography, AP World History, Accounting 1 Award, AP Environmental Science, National Honors Society, Student Board Member

College: 2026 Commit to Belmont University

My Quote About Janell: "JJ was a beam of light in my life. She is one of the main reasons I am where I am today. She was the first person to give me hope that girls' college golf is possible. She was the older sister I never had who I knew I could always go to for advice. She was fully a part of our family. I will always be grateful for the impact she had on my life, and I hope to carry her love of golf through the rest of my life."

Braden Gillespie

High School: 2024 Tennessean Schooldays Champion (100th Annual Tournament)...Two-time TSSAA Individual District II-A Champion... TSSAA Individual State Finalist...Three-time Notah Begay Championship Regional Finalist...Drive, Chip, and Putt Sub-Regional Champion... Two-time Mid-South Golf Player of the Year...14 Junior tournament titles...Academic and leadership accomplishments including Honor Roll and High School Leadership Team

College: 2026 Commit to Freed-Hardeman University

My Quote About Janell: "JJ was truly a reflection of God's love, kindness, and grace. She had such an impact on not only me but everyone she interacted with. She will always be in our hearts and will forever be missed."

Lane Walton

High School: Ranked 30th for the Class of 2025 for the state of Tennessee...Varsity team advanced to District and Region Tournaments his junior year, and he received honors for finishing in top 5/90. Placed 7th in Region tournament...Finalist in School Days Tournament...Ten first place finishes in sophomore and junior years...Wilson Cup, placed 3rd his sophomore year and advanced to District and Region Tournaments, finalist in District Tournament, out of 50 players.

freshman year: Advanced to District and Region tournaments and District Champion runner up...in 2023 qualified for Tennessee Amateur, one of 7 qualifiers out of 160 in 16-year age group.

College: Freed-Hardeman University

My Quote About Janell: "Coach JJ always told me if you don't have your best stuff today, just grind it out and find a way to win."

Acknowledgements

This page of acknowledgments is not an afterthought but a true declaration of my thanks and appreciation to people who have not only impacted my journey but helped me write about the journey of Janell. I am so grateful for their influence in my life and the inspiration they provide to me.

First, thank You, God, for saving me not only at the young age of 7 but also during a crucible moment in my life. Through Jesus, I am forever grateful for the opportunity to have a relationship with You and to share Your Kingdom principles to people in need on Earth. You are my Father, my Rock, and the Author of my moments! Thanks for giving me the title of this book, the words to write, and the inspiration to tell this incredible story. I know You will use this book to impact people in their journey and to help them make the most of their moments. My prayer is that they would discover You along the way!

Thanks so much to my wife Gina! You have truly inspired me, and I am so grateful for all of the moments we have shared together as a couple and as parents raising five sons. Your passion for life is contagious, your talents are incredible, and your ability to connect with people, especially with junior high students, is admirable and inspiring. Thank you for your love and support through the years, and I look forward to continuing to co-lead our ever-expanding family with you and making even more special memories along the way!

Thanks to Drew, Will, Kyle, Ben, and Grant, our five-son basketball team. I am so grateful to God for each of you. Thanks for letting me coach you in so many sports over the years. Many of the principles in this book were forged and refined in the heat of competition during our time together on the field and on the court. Most of all, I am so glad I get to be your father, and I am always here for you.

I am also grateful to Dr. David Cook, the man who breathed life into my dreams and continues to be a close friend, mentor, and colleague. Thanks for showing me the way and for always encouraging me to pursue God's best for my life. You are a true inspiration, and many lives have been impacted because of your investment in me.

Thanks to Donna and Chuck Lysack for reaching out to schedule a coaching session with Janell, one that would lead to many special moments and memories along the way. Thank you for trusting me to coach her and for entrusting me with the privilege of telling her story!

Thanks to my mom for raising me as a single mom and for instilling in me the gift and power of written and spoken words. Thank you also for serving as one of the editors and reviewers of this book as it was being shaped and refined. Most of all, thank you for living out your faith and for being a prayer warrior for me and so many others.

Thanks to Terrence Gee, who has served as a mentor, colleague, and close friend throughout my entire professional life. The way things are going, we will probably spend our remaining time on earth doing work and life together until it's time to move on to our eternal home in Heaven. For that, I am deeply grateful.

To all the athletes, parents, coaches, and teams that have invited me to be a part of their lives and journeys, thank you. I have learned so much from every encounter, and it has been a joy to share these championship mindset principles with you and to watch you grow and flourish.

Thanks to my publishing team including Catherine King and Amanda Blake who helped make this book even better than I could have imagined. Catherine, I so appreciated your editing expertise and insightful feedback to help me refine my message. Amanda, you did an incredible job with the design of this book including the book cover, which connects a name, a face, and a journey!

Finally, thank you, the reader, for choosing this book. My prayer is that it will have a meaningful impact on your life, inspire you to live with greater purpose on your own journey, and encourage you to make the most of your moments.

About the Author

Mike Van Hoozer is an expert in the psychology of human performance, serving as a mental performance coach and leadership consultant for elite athletes and global business leaders. As the founder of Van Hoozer and Associates and Life Beyond Athletics, he has helped thousands of athletes and leaders master their "mental game" to achieve peak performance and build a resilient mindset. His clients include professional NFL and MLB players, high school and college athletes, coaches, and teams across all sports, Fortune 500 executives and companies, non-profit organizations, and churches.

A former senior executive with Accenture and a graduate of Baylor University, Mike is the author of several books, including *Moments: Making Your Life Count For What Matters Most* and *Be Present: Showing Up When It Matters Most*. Mike hosts a popular podcast and has delivered his *Invisible Hand of Leadership* program to thousands of leaders worldwide. *The Journey of Janell* represents his latest work in exploring the intersection of grit, grace, and a life lived on purpose for a purpose. Mike is an endurance athlete and Boston Marathon qualifier who lives in Texas with his wife, Gina, where he serves as the "coach" to their five sons.

Janell Lysack Joslin Foundation

Janell's family created the Janell Lysack Joslin Foundation to honor Janell and her compassion for community outreach as well as her desire to enrich the lives of those younger than her. This foundation is a 501.c.3 non-profit organization that supports community outreach in programs Janell was involved in throughout her life. These efforts include scholarships for high school students continuing their education, community outreach programs, development programs for junior golfers, and support programs for military home front groups.

You can learn more and donate to the foundation using this link:

janelllysackjoslinfoundation.org

or scan this Donation QR code:

The foundation also hosts an annual fundraising golf tournament in collaboration with Meadowbrook Farms Golf Club in Katy, TX, where she played many rounds of golf in her life and where her presence is still felt today. You can learn more about the tournament and how to sign up in the Events section of the web site.

Notes

INTRODUCTION

1. Sean Curran, "All Praise." Lyrics by Steffany Gretzinger / Daniel Bashta / Sean Curran / Dante Bowe.

2. Dr. David Cook, *greatness* (Marcelin, MO: Walsworth Publishing Company, 2021), 89–90.

CHAPTER 2: THE MEETING

1. **Miles in *The Equalizer 2* Movie**: Director: Antoine Fuqua, Sony Pictures, 2018.

CHAPTER 4: FOCUS ON WHAT YOU CAN CONTROL

1. Craig Groeschel, *Winning The War In Your Mind* (Grand Rapids, Michigan: Zondervan Books, 2021), 1.

CHAPTER 5: BE OUTCOME-DRIVEN AND PROCESS-FOCUSED

1. Jon Gordon, *The One Truth: Elevate Your Mind, Unlock Your Power, Heal Your Soul* (Hoboken, NJ: Wiley, 2023).

2. Dr. David Cook, quote from his greatness Live Conference in Fredericksburg, TX, November, 2024.

CHAPTER 6: DEVELOP AN I WILL MINDSET

1. Jon Gordon: Reference regarding loving the process to love the results.

2. Steve Magness, *Do Hard Things* (New York, NY: HarperOne, 2022) 128.

3. Dr. Bob Rotella, *Golf is Not a Game of Perfect* (New York, NY: Simon and Schuster, 1995).

4. Rebekah Lyons: Quote post on Instagram (2026) regarding how thoughts shape perspective and attitude.

CHAPTER 7: JANELL'S JUNIOR YEAR

1. Mike Van Hoozer, *Moments: Making Your Life Count For What Matters Most* (Sevierville, TN: Insight Publishing, 2006), xiii.

2. Stephen R. Covey, *The Seven Habits of Highly Effective People* (New York, NY: Simon and Schuster, 1989, 2004, 2020), 78.

3. Fulton Oursler: Quote regarding the "two thieves" of regret and fear.

4. *Tyler Perry*: Quote regarding how life moments change one's trajectory.

CHAPTER 9: A CRUCIBLE MOMENT

1. Dr. Caroline Leaf: "Healthy Ways to Process Grief" podcast, February 27, 2022.

2. Louie Giglio **Life Interrupted Series**: "Death Interrupted" talk.

CHAPTER 10: 68

1. Jon Gordon: Quote regarding the "leap of faith" on Instagram post, January, 2025.

CHAPTER 11: DAY 2

1. Dr. David Cook, *Seven Days in Utopia* (Grand Rapids, MI: Zondervan, 2011), 109.

2. Jerry Sittser, *A Grace Disguised: How The Soul Grows Through Loss* (Grand Rapids, Michigan: Zondervan, 2021), 93.

CHAPTER 12: MOMENTS THAT MATTER

1. C. William Pollard: Quote regarding the measurement of a servant leader's results from his speech: "The Leader Who Serves, Windsor, UK, April 23, 1994.

EPILOGUE: THE FINAL CHAPTER

1. *The Last Samurai Movie*: Director: Edward Zwick, (Warner Bros. 2003). Dialogue regarding how a person lived versus how they died.

2. Christine Caine: Quote regarding living every day with purpose on Instagram, 2026.

Bring This Message of Grit and Grace to Your Team!

Whether you are leading a corporate team, a sports team, or a school, church, or non-profit organization, *The Journey of Janell* provides a framework for mental performance and resilient leadership. We offer specialized pricing for bulk purchases of **25 copies or more**.

BULK BENEFITS:

- **Tiered Discounts:** Significant savings off the retail price.
- **Signed Copies:** Exclusive signed editions by Mike Van Hoozer (subject to availability).
- **Integrated Training:** Orders of 100+ copies may be eligible for additional perks including a complimentary 30-minute virtual Q&A session with your group.

To purchase bulk copies of *The Journey of Janell* for large groups or teambuilding and leadership events for your company or organization or to book Mike to come bring this message to your team, please email mike@mikevanhoozer.com and either Mike or a team member will follow up with you.

ADDITIONAL RESOURCES

If you are interested in programs and coaching for you and your team on leadership and performance in sports, business, and life, contact us at:

Email: mike@mikevanhoozer.com

Web Site: www.mikevanhoozer.com

or by using this QR Code, which includes my social media platforms:

9 798994 867327